MUSTANG

AMERICA'S PONYCAR

BY THE EDITORS OF CONSUMER GUIDE® AUTOMOTIVE

Publications International, Ltd.

Louis Weber, CEO
Publications International, Ltd.
7373 North Cicero Avenue
Lincolnwood, Illinois 60712

ISBN-13: 978-1-4508-2687-7
ISBN-10: 1-4508-2687-3

Manufactured in China.

8 7 6 5 4 3 2 1

Library of Congress Control Number: 2011925347

Credits

Photography

The editors would like to thank the following people and organizations for supplying the photography that made this book possible. They are listed below, along with the page number(s) of their photos:

Darrel Arment: 37; **Mark Bilek:** 136; **Jeff Cohn:** 177, 181, 182, 183, 185, 186; **Chuck Giametta:** 163; **Thomas Glatch:** 65; **Sam Griffith:** 51, 118, 121; **David Hogan:** 134; **Dan Lyons:** 38, 54, 60, 61; **Vince Manocchi:** 13, 20, 22, 23, 26, 49, 50, 66, 81, 153; **Doug Mitchel:** 39, 78, 108, 138, 141, 146, 150; **Mike Mueller:** 33, 40, 55; **David Newhardt:** 14, 16, 17, 19, 22, 23, 47, 53; **Rick Popely:** 134; **Steve Statham:** 62; **Nicky Wright:** 27, 34, 35, 36, 41, 52, 63, 68, 105

Front cover: Ron Kimball/www.kimballstock.com

Foreword: David Newhardt

Chapter Opener Illustrations by Frank Peiler: 9, 29, 43, 57, 71, 83, 97, 111, 127, 143, 159, 175

Owners

Special thanks to the owners of the cars featured in this book for their cooperation. Their names and the page number(s) for their vehicles follow:

Steve Ames: 55; **Robert Augustine:** 54; **Dennis Begley:** 41; **Jim Buhle:** 69; **Tim Carie:** 50; **Luis A. Chanes:** 47; **Charles and Marie Cobb:** 36; **Dr. Randy and Freda Cooper:** 26; **Gary Emerson:** 39; **Richard A. Emry:** 27; **George and Tony Gloriosa:** 78; **Steve Grant:** 13; **Gary Gumushian:** 68; **Tom Haase:** 46; **Keith Hazely:** 41; **Lewis H. Hunter:** 51; **Teresa and Doug Hvidston:** 105; **Tony Kanzia:** 118; **Don and Karen Kerridge:** 63; **Leroy Lasiter:** 52; **Mitch Lindahl:** 108; **Bruce Meyers:** 22, 23; **Erin O'Neill:** 14; **Charles Plylar:** 40; **Pat Price:** 22, 23; **John Prokop:** 53; **Brian Sbardelli:** 81; **Albert Schildknecht:** 16, 17; **Schmerler Ford:** 121; **Daniel Schmitt and Co.:** 37; **Southwest Gallery of Cars:** 62; **Allan St. Jacques:** 19; **Frank Trummer:** 65; **Mike Venarde:** 49; **Ed and Debbie Werder:** 33; **Edward Wey:** 38; **Ernest Wheeler:** 20; **Ron Wold:** 34, 35

Our appreciation to the historical archives and media services groups at Ford Motor Company.

About The Editors of Consumer Guide®:

For more than 40 years, Consumer Guide® has been a trusted provider of new-car buying information.

The Consumer Guide® staff drives and evaluates more than 200 vehicles annually.

Consumerguide.com is one of the web's most popular automotive resources, visited by roughly three million shoppers monthly.

The Editors of Consumer Guide® also publish the award-winning bimonthly *Collectible Automobile®* magazine.

CONTENTS

FOREWORD

It was one of Ford's best ideas: a simple, low-cost small car offering sporty style, a youthful driving spirit, and personal features to suit any taste and budget. Mustang was a smash hit from the day it was unveiled in April 1964, and it's still going strong today. That's almost 50 years of uninterrupted production, a status that few cars in the world have achieved.

That incredible feat becomes even more impressive when one considers how much the world has changed since the mid-1960s. The secret? Mustang keeps changing with the times, but its timeless personality doesn't. Mustang has always been about fun and adventure for both the young and young-at-heart. Always will be. No wonder it's been loved by so many for so long.

Today's Mustangs are sophisticated machines that deliver the cutting-edge luxury, convenience, and performance features that modern-day buyers demand, but with an undeniable charisma and a colorful heritage that few contemporary cars can match. The skilled Ford Motor Company engineers and designers who are tasked with creating the Mustangs of tomorrow are well aware of the car's legacy, and their responsibility to uphold it. They know, along with the scores of fervent Mustang fans around the world, that Mustang is much more than just another car. They realize they are caretakers of a legend.

Mustang is one of history's greatest automotive success stories, and it started a true automotive revolution. This book celebrates the iconic, all-American breed that keeps galloping into the future at full speed while never losing sight of the past. Enjoy!

1

Mustang thundered onto America's automotive landscape like no car in history, captivating the nation to capture a million sales in its first model year alone. Thanks to a mile-long options list, the Mustang could be almost anything to anybody—the ultimate "personal" car.

1964–1966: OUT OF THE GATE

Automakers are old hands at promoting their wares, and are particularly adept at baiting the press. An information leak here, an "unauthorized" photo there—voila!—instant publicity. Ford utilized these tricks in early Mustang promotion and went one better on the evening of April 16, 1964, with the purchase of commercial time during the 9 P.M. slot on all three television networks; an estimated 29 million viewers were treated to the Mustang's unveiling without ever leaving their living rooms. The next morning, 2600 American newspapers carried announcement ads and articles. As the capper, Ford arranged for Mustang to be officially introduced at the April 17 opening of the New York World's Fair.

The publicity mill continued to grind as some 150 newspaper and magazine journalists were invited to Detroit to drive virtually hand-built

Mustangs. The scribes raved about the car, and Mustangs quickly went on display in airport terminals, hotel lobbies, and dealer showrooms across the country. Base price was boldly advertised everywhere. And why not? At just $2368 for the hardtop, the Mustang was a tremendous bargain.

Long before all this, Ford had projected first-year Mustang sales of 100,000 units. As announcement day approached, Lee Iacocca upped the estimate to 240,000 and switched his division's San Jose, California, plant to Mustang production. Iacocca had been conservative: Only four months were needed to sell 100,000 Mustangs. For the full 1965 model run—April 1964 through August 1965—a total of 680,989 were sold, an all-time industry record for first-year sales. By March 1966, the one-millionth Mustang had rolled off the line.

Most automotive experts greeted the Mustang with qualified enthusiasm, which partly reflected the nature of the car. Underneath that striking new shape was little more than just another Detroit compact— and a humble Falcon at that. But most critics were willing to forgive this, because performance and handling equipment was available to make any Mustang a competent grand tourer.

Standard equipment on the early "1964½" models included the 170-cubic-inch Falcon six, 3-speed manual floorshift transmission, full wheel covers, padded dash, bucket seats, and carpeting. From there, you were on your own with the very robust options list. A sampling: Cruise-O-Matic, 4-speed manual, or 3-speed overdrive transmissions (around $180 depending on engine); three V-8s ($106–$328); limited-slip differential ($42); Rally-Pac (tachometer and clock, $69); power brakes ($42); front disc brakes (from late 1965 on, non-assisted, $58); deluxe steering wheel ($32); power steering ($84); air conditioning (except with the "Hi-Performance" V-8); full-length center console ($50); vinyl roof covering for the hardtop ($74); push-button AM radio with antenna ($58); knock-off-style wheel covers ($18 for the set); 14-inch wire wheel covers ($45) and styled steel wheels (with V-8 only, $120); and a profusion of tires (including whitewalls and larger rubber up to 6.95 X 14).

Opposite page: The Mustang began in 1961 as Project T-5, which produced scores of styling ideas, including the mock-up shown at top left. The Mustang name wasn't decided on until almost the 11th hour; note the Cougar insignia and grille emblems on the coupe styling study and convertible prototype shown here. *This page:* Unveiled in October 1963, the "experimental" Mustang II was actually the fully engineered production Mustang with exaggerated nose and tail styling, a cut-down windshield, custom lift-off hardtop, and jazzy "show car" interior. It kicked off a carefully orchestrated publicity buildup to the showroom Mustang's debut. *Above:* Henry Ford II poses with the 1964$\frac{1}{2}$ Mustang at New York World's Fair on April 17, 1964, the day of its public unveiling.

Buyers could also select option *packages:* Visibility Group (mirrors and wipers, $36); Accent Group (pinstriping and rocker panel moldings, $27); special handling package (for V-8s only, $31); Instrument Group (needle gauges for fuel, water, oil pressure, and amperes, plus round speedometer, $109); and a GT Group (disc brakes, driving lights, and special trim, $165). The most expensive single option, air conditioning, listed at a reasonable $283, and many of the more desirable individual items—such as the $107 "Pony" Interior Decor Group with horses embroidered on the seat backs—were well within the reach of most buyers.

Engine options played a big role in determining a Mustang's personality. During the long 20-month 1965 model run, powerplant offerings were shuffled slightly. The original standard engine, the 101-hp Falcon six, was dropped after September 1964 (considered the accepted break between "1964½" and the "true" 1965 models). Its replacement was a 200-cid six with 120 hp. The 200 was an improvement on the 170 because of its higher compression, redesigned valvetrain, and seven (instead of five) main bearings. It also featured an automatic choke, short-stroke cylinder block for longer piston and cylinder wear, hydraulic valve lifters, and an intake manifold integral with the head.

The smallest V-8 initially offered was the modern 260-cid "thinwall" unit from the Fairlane, rated at 164 hp. A bore enlarged from 3.80 to 4.00 inches made it a 289 (on the same 2.87-inch stroke), offering 195 hp with the two-barrel carburetor or 210 hp with an optional four-barrel carb (for an additional $158). A "Hi-Performance" (HP) four-barrel version delivered 271 hp; price was $276 with the GT Group, $328 without. After September 1964, the 260 was discontinued and a 200-hp, two-barrel 289 became the base V-8 option (at $106). Output of the standard four-barrel unit was then boosted to 225 hp, while the "Hi-Po" version was unchanged.

The four-barrel engines achieved their extra power by increased carburetor air velocity matched to the engine's performance curve. They also had valve timing different from that of the two-barrel engines, plus a higher compression ratio that demanded premium fuel.

This page: Ford kept up the promotional pace in the months after Mustang's launch. A highlight was the new pony's selection as pace car for the 1964 Indianapolis 500, where a convertible did the honors. Henry Ford's grandson Benson Ford piloted the pace car; he is shown behind the wheel here, with the famous Borg-Warner Trophy in the background. Note the pace car's windshield-mounted grab handle and unique "gold-stripe" whitewall tires. A. J. Foyt took the '64 race's checkered flag in an Offenhauser-powered roadster, marking the last time a front-engined race car won at the 500. *Opposite page:* Ford Division chief Lee Iacocca ordered that pace-car-replica coupes be built as an incentive for top-selling Ford dealers. Approximately 190 were made, all finished in Wimbledon White with graphics that matched the pace-car convertible. All were equipped with the 260-cubic-inch V-8, automatic transmission, power steering, AM radio, and back-up lights. Few survive today.

Ordering the Hi-Performance 289 meant buyers also had to take the extra-cost 4-speed gearbox, which made the latter a "mandatory option"—a contradiction in terms but an arrangement much-beloved by Detroit automakers in the Sixties. The HP was also the only engine offered with optional "short" rear axle ratios (3.89:1 and 4.11:1) favored by drag racers. Standard ratios were 3.20:1 with the six, 2.80:1 with the two-barrel V-8, 3.00:1 with the four-barrel V-8, and 3.50:1 with the HP.

For real performance, of course, buyers could spring for the most "special" of Mustangs: the GT-350 Shelby Cobra. A creation of Carroll Shelby—a lanky Texan who had been a roustabout, a chicken farmer, and a champion driver—the GT-350 was instigated by Ford, which was looking for a car capable of whipping Corvettes in Sports Car Club of America (SCCA) B-Production competition. Shelby's participation also brought the Cobra name, which had rocketed to prominence beginning in 1962, when Shelby dropped a Ford 289 into a lightweight AC Ace roadster and called it the AC/Shelby Cobra.

Final specs for the GT-350 were determined by the fall of 1964, and a dozen cars were subsequently built by hand at Shelby's small production facility in Venice, California. In addition, 88 of 100 production Mustangs shipped by Ford to Venice for homologation purposes had been transformed by New Year's Day, 1965. The GT-350 was unveiled at Riverside Raceway on January 27, 1965.

The "full-strength" GT-350R (R for "racing") was conceived as a competition car; the street GT-350 was simply a less extreme, more tractable version of it. A beefed-up suspension that included a steel brace running between the shock towers improved handling and limited body flex. Rolling stock comprised hefty 15 X 6-inch wheels shod with 7.75 X 15 Goodyear Blue Dot performance tires.

Underhood modifications included aluminum high-rise manifolds, wilder camshaft profile, and a larger Holley carburetor fed by a functional scoop in a hood made of fiberglass instead of steel. These changes, plus a less restrictive exhaust system, boosted the HP 289 to an honest 306

Opposite page, left: The Mustang convertible struts its stuff in one of two photos used for announcement-week ads. *Right:* Even no-frills models were quite dressy, as vinyl bucket seats, carpeting, and wheel covers were all included. *This page, top left:* Mustang fast eclipsed the all-time first-year sales record set by Ford's own 1960 Falcon. This PR photo shows the popular duo flanking division executives Donald Frey (left) and Lee Iacocca. *Above:* The hottest engine available on regular Mustangs was the 271-hp "Hi-Performance" 289 V-8. It cost $328 on non-GT models, and a four-speed manual transmission was a mandatory extra. *Left:* The Mustang cut an undeniably dashing profile. Styling was handsome and well-proportioned, with crisp body lines accented by just the right amount of chrome-trim detail.

Both pages: Mustang caused more buyer excitement than any Ford in a generation. The terrific styling was one big reason. Almost everyone loved it—even hard-boiled critics. Small front-fender emblems, as on this hardtop, identified cars with one of four optional V-8 engines, which initially ranged from a 160-hp 260 to the 271-hp 289. This Phoenician Yellow example is equipped with the 195-hp two-barrel 289.

horsepower. (The competition version was tweaked even more, to 340–360 gross horsepower.)

All 1965 GT-350s were painted white; no other colors were available. All Ford and Mustang badging and insignia were removed, but the blue rocker-panel stripes prominently displayed the GT-350 name. The back seat was removed, but Shelby offered a bolt-on bench kit for useful "+2" seating.

The street GT-350 went for $4547, about $1500 more than a standard V-8 Mustang. From a standing start, 60 mph came up in an average of 6.5 seconds. Top speed was 130–135 mph, and the car handled like a true race machine. And at $5950, the competition-only R version was a real bargain capable of going directly from showroom to winner's circle.

Although the Shelby was not an easy car to drive, demand for the street version quickly exceeded the capability of Carroll Shelby's facility, prompting Shelby-American, Inc., to move from Venice to two huge hangars at Los Angeles International Airport in the spring of 1965.

Meanwhile, the "regular" Mustang continued to evolve. Front disc brakes built by Kelsey-Hayes were offered beginning late in the '65 model year, and a new model came along, too: a snazzy Mustang coupe with semi-fastback styling that arrived with the rest of the '65 Ford line in autumn 1964. Several names were considered, including GT Limited, Grand Sport, and, ironically, GTO, but the final nameplates read "2+2." That was apt, because rear leg room was scant—even less than in the hardtop or convertible. But there was compensation in an optional fold-down rear seat, with a partition in the trunk bulkhead that dropped forward to create a long load platform that could accommodate skis or fishing rods. Instead of rear-quarter windows, the 2+2 had gill-like C-pillar air vents, part of the flow-through ventilation system.

The first Mustang was undeniably attractive, but the fact remains that it was more an example of brilliant marketing than a piece of revolutionary design and engineering. The body carried too many non-functional "gingerbread" touches, and utilization of interior space, given the 108-inch wheelbase, wasn't exactly a model of practicality.

With standard suspension, Mustang offered a wallowing, sometimes floaty ride that fell short of the car's sporting pretensions. The 210-hp 4-speed managed the 0–60 sprint in nine seconds, performance that failed to impress *Road & Track*. The magazine's opinion changed radically, though, when a tester laid hands on a 271-hp Hi-Performance V-8 and took it from rest to 60 mph in 8.3 seconds. *Motor Trend* made the same run in 7.6 seconds.

The HP engine was good, but changes wrought by the optional and inexpensive handling package were even more impressive. Stiff springs and shocks, a large-diameter front anti-sway bar, 5.90 X 15 Firestone Super Sports tires, and a quicker steering ratio (3.5 turns lock-to-lock) brought

This page: Mustang's early sales pace was too much for Ford's River Rouge plant, so production was added to two other factories. For the full 1965 model-year run, an amazing 680,989 Mustangs were sold, setting an industry record for first-year sales. Note the two factory-fresh Ford Falcons in this photo; Mustangs were assembled alongside Falcons since the two shared their basic underpinnings. Opposite page: This Honey Gold 1965 convertible carries several highly desirable options, including a 289 V-8, "Rally Pac" tachometer/clock combo, air conditioning, styled steel wheels, and the GT Equipment Group with grille-mounted driving lights, special emblems, racing stripes, and more.

Both pages: After a six-month run of "1964½" Mustangs, Ford adjusted standard equipment and added more options for "true" '65 models that started sale in September 1964. Among them was the planned 2+2 semi-fastback coupe with a racy roofline featuring single side windows ahead of gill-like air-extractor vents, part of an exclusive flow-through ventilation system. The 2+2 pipped the convertible as the second-most popular body style for the formal 1965 model year.

noticeably improved roadworthiness. The ride was occasionally harsh but firm enough to inspire driver confidence, despite a marked degree of oversteer (the tendency of rear wheels to lose traction and skid sideways in a turn).

Mustang seemed born to race, and did so even before it went on sale. In late winter of 1963–64, Ford prepped a team of rally Mustangs to take over for the newly banned Falcon Sprints in European events. The effort was sincere enough, but the team's only major win came in the Tour de France, where Peter Proctor and Peter Harper finished one-two in class.

More success was found on the dragstrips, where 2+2s stuffed full of Ford's 427-cid big-block racked up numerous wins in NHRA's A/FX class and, less often, as "funny cars." The factory jumped into the fray for the '65

season, fielding wild "altereds" with two-inch-shorter wheelbases. And—not unexpectedly—Carroll Shelby's GT-350s tore up the tracks (and more than a few Corvettes) in SCCA B-Production-class events.

With Mustang sales roaring along as the 1966 model year approached, Ford product planners saw little reason to tamper with success. Though the '66 looked like a '65 rerun at first glance, there were a few changes.

Up front, the honeycomb grille texture was replaced by thin bars, and the thick horizontal chrome bar was discarded, leaving the galloping horse to float in its chromed rectangular frame. Mustang GTs kept the grille bar, however, with auxiliary driving lights mounted at the ends. At the rear was a restyled fuel filler cap. Along the sides, the simulated rear-wheel scoop was decorated with three windsplits (except on GTs, 2+2s, and luxury models, which didn't have this trim). Front fender nameplates and emblems were revised, and the stock wheel covers were redesigned.

Both pages: **Bowing in January 1965, the GT-350 was a special high-performance 2+2 conceived and built at Ford's behest by Carroll Shelby of Cobra sports-car fame. The desired Corvette-beater featured a 306-hp "Cobra-tuned" V-8, track-ready chassis, and weight-saving tricks like omitting the rear seat. Bigger wheels, tires, and brakes were installed, as were bold strips and racing seatbelts. Upper-front control arms were relocated and lowered, and override rear traction bars were added. The no-compromise modifications made the GT-350 rawer and more uncivilized than many customers could handle, at least as an everyday driver. They were also pricey at $4457, which limited their sales primarily to hardcore enthusiasts—just 562 GT-350s were produced for 1965.**

comparable 12-month periods, the '66s actually ran ahead by 50,000 units. Mustang still had no direct competition and romped along at close to half a million hardtops, 70,000 convertibles, and 35,000 fastbacks.

Though it looked very much like its V-8 counterpart, the six-cylinder Mustang—which was vigorously promoted by Ford—was considerably different. Its wheels had only four lugs, while V-8 models had five. All Mustangs had standard drum brakes, but sixes had good-performing nine-inchers, V-8s 10-inchers. The six-cylinder cars also had a lighter rear axle and a slightly narrower front track, and their spring rates were somewhat lower to keep an even keel; had they used the heavier V-8 suspension, they would have appeared tail-heavy.

The Mustang six performed reasonably well for a car of its class. *Motor Trend*'s automatic-equipped model ran 0–60 mph in 14.3 seconds and averaged 20 mpg on regular gas. Existing at the other end of the performance spectrum was the Shelby Cobra GT-350, made smoother and less raw for '66. Color choices expanded, and the fastback's extra-cost fold-down rear seat became a Shelby option as well. Automatic

Inside, alterations were more functional. For example, the original Falcon-style instrument cluster with its old-fashioned strip speedometer was replaced by the five-gauge unit with the round speedo previously reserved for the GT package. The column-mounted Rally-Pac tachometer/clock combination remained on the option list.

Changes to running gear included an upgrade of six-cylinder models from 13- to 14-inch wheels and, for all models, reworked engine mounts to reduce vibration. Engine choices remained at four: the standard 200-cid six and the three optional 289s. The already generous option list was extended to include a stereo 8-track tape player ($128) and deluxe seatbelts ($15).

Predictably, Mustang's 1966 sales were down compared to model-year '65, which was longer than usual due to the early introduction. But for

Opposite page: A thin-bar grille with "floating" polo pony was one of the few styling changes for 1966. Separate taillamps had been considered during the original design effort but were precluded by their higher cost. The idea resurfaced on prototype '66s (as seen in these early press photos) but didn't make production, again to hold down prices. *This page:* Even six-cylinder-powered Mustangs like this Arcadian Blue coupe could be optioned with the steering-column mounted Rally Pac gauges. Wire-wheel-look wheel covers added a classy, upscale vibe. Mustang sales for the year dipped slightly, to 607,568.

transmission was made an option—hardly the thing to excite driving enthusiasts. However, a Paxton centrifugal supercharger was another new option, sold factory-installed for $670 or as a $430 kit. Ford claimed that the blower boosted horsepower by 46 percent, to more than 400 hp. Zero-to-60 times were cut to five seconds. These were potent cars that enjoyed considerable success in 1966 Trans-Am racing and in SCCA events.

Total 1966 Shelby Mustang production was 2380, including 936 Hertz models and six specially built convertibles Carroll gave to friends. (In addition, 252 leftover '65 GT-350s were updated to 1966 specs.)

The public's enthusiasm for the whole range of Mustangs made Ford well aware that competitors were readying ponycars of their own, but this had little to do with the more substantial changes that were already in the works for '67 Mustang. These had been initiated in mid-1964, just as the country was catching "Mustang Fever," and reflected the industry's usual three-year lead time, the ritual of annual style changes, and, to some extent, Ford's uncertainty at that point about how the original concept would "play in Peoria."

So the '67 Mustang was a bolder and brawnier model that started Ford's lithe ponycar down the path toward a bigger-is-better mentality, a seven-year journey that would ultimately lead Ford and Mustang back to square one.

This page, top: **The '66s got slightly tidier detailing around the nose but were otherwise hard to tell from '65s at a glance.** *Bottom:* **This well-equipped '66 2+2 shows off the GT package's rocker-panel stripes and bright exhaust tips.** *Opposite page:* **The 1966 Shelby GT-350H was the result of a 1965 agreement between Hertz Rent-a-Car, Shelby-American, and Ford. The "H" stood for Hertz, of course. For $17 a day and 17 cents a mile, Hertz customers (who had to be at least 25 years old and members of Hertz's Sports Car Club) could rent a genuine Shelby Mustang. Most of the cars were black with gold stripes, but a few were painted Candy Apple Red with gold stripes. The special-order cars were a big production and profit booster for Shelby, but Hertz abandoned the program because many customers went on unauthorized track outings, which often damaged the cars and lost Hertz a pile of money.**

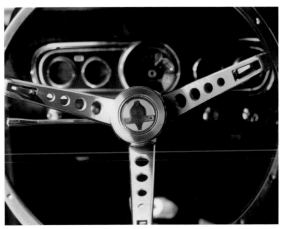

2

How do you follow a million-seller in Detroit? Make it even better. Ford did just that with the 1967 Mustang, adding a fresh "performance" look and go-power to match. A good thing, too, because rival manufacturers were now answering Mustang with ponycars of their own.

1967–1968: ALL DELIBERATE SPEED

Mustang's instant success raised vexing questions when work on the follow-up '67s began in mid-1964. Though planners knew some changes would be needed, they weren't sure at first what those ought to be. It was also unclear how archrival Chevrolet would respond. As engineer Tom Feaheny told author Gary Witzenburg: "It was a long ways down the road before we were aware that they were coming after us." As we know, Chevy's response was a strong one: the new-for-'67 Camaro.

Beyond this "was an opportunity to do a lot of refinement work," as Feaheny put it. "Frankly, the amount of engineering in that [first Mustang] was not as great as it could have been…." Feaheny also noted that product planning chief Hal Sperlich wanted to "one-up the original in every respect…." The mid-1964 arrival of Pontiac's GTO muscle car influenced development too; Ford figured that even a ponycar could always use more deliberate speed in the burgeoning horsepower race.

In the end, the '67 Mustang retained its predecessor's basic chassis, inner structure, and running gear, but was different most everywhere else. The big news was a planned big-inch V-8: the 390 "Thunderbird Special" with four-barrel carburetor and a rousing 320 horsepower. As a Mustang option it cost $264, versus $434 for the "Hi-Po" 271-hp 289 small-block. Also new was three-speed "SelectShift" Cruise-O-Matic transmission ($233) with a manual gear-hold feature for maximum acceleration. Other powertrains were basically unchanged: 120-hp 200-cubic-inch six and 200- and 225-hp 289 V-8s with stick or automatic transmission.

The 390 made for a very front-heavy Mustang (58 percent of total curb weight) that understeered with abandon. Though the option included F70-14 Wide Oval tires to help counter that, most everyone said small-block Mustangs handled better. Big-block buyers were well advised to order the $389 Competition Handling Package, though that meant ponying

up for the GT option too. Also available with the HP 289, the "comp" package delivered stiffer springs/front stabilizer bar, Koni adjustable shocks, limited-slip axle, quick-ratio steering, and 15-inch wheels, all of which improved handling at the expense of ride comfort—which may be why few buyers ordered it. Of course, the big-block's big payoff was terrific acceleration: typically 7.5 seconds 0–60 mph, 15.5 at 95 mph in the standing quarter-mile, and close to 120 mph flat out.

Mustang looked more muscular for '67, thanks to a lower-body restyle featuring a concave back panel with separate triple taillamps (finally!), more rear-fender hop-up, and a longer nose with a larger grille and no flanking "gills." A new extra-cost Exterior Decor Group added thin horizontal bars to the back panel and twin dummy hood scoops with turn-signal indicator lights. Combining the GT option with automatic transmission changed front-fender badging to "GT/A." In addition, the 2+2 coupe went from semi-notchback to a sweeping full fastback roofline. The convertible sported an articulated-glass rear window with a horizontal crease that allowed it to "bend" as the top folded.

Wheelbase was unchanged, but overall length grew two inches (to 183.6), width by 2.7 inches (to 70.9), and front track by 2.6 inches. The last was done chiefly to make room for the bulky 390 V-8, but it improved handling on any '67. So did various front-suspension tweaks borrowed from Carroll Shelby's GT-350.

The '67s shed another vestige of Mustang's Falcon origins with a unique new "twin-cowl" dashboard dominated by a pair of large, circular dials ahead of the driver. Among useful new options were the Tilt-Away steering wheel from recent Thunderbirds and a "Convenience Control Panel" warning-light array.

Though the '67 Mustang compared well with Chevy's Camaro and a reworked Plymouth Barracuda, the new ponycar competition (which also included corporate-cousin Mercury Cougar) took a toll on model-year sales, which plunged some 25 percent from the '66 tally. But 472,121 orders was hardly bad, and Mustang bested Camaro by more than two to one.

This page: **Mustang had just left the corral when work on the follow-up '67 model began in mid-1964 at the Ford Division studio under Gale Halderman. A four-sedan clay model (shown here) was mocked-up, then discarded as "un-Mustang."** *Opposite page, top left:* **The basic '67 shape and proportions began to emerge in October 1964. This life-size clay shows ideas for bodyside and back-panel contouring.** *Top right:* **Photographed in January 1965, this full-size 2+2 was one of many mock-ups given the executive eye in the Ford Design Center's curtained showroom. At a glance it's very close to the final '67, but the upper bodyside character line would be abbreviated, and the triple rear-roof vent doors wouldn't make it.** *Bottom right:* **Wide, louvered taillamps were rejected too.** *Bottom left:* **Many design elements were locked in by early November 1964, but some, such as bodyside scoops, were not.**

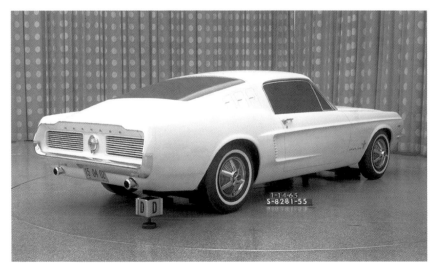

Opposite page: All 1967 Mustangs got new lower-body sheetmetal designed to suggest stronger performance, but the 2+2 also got a sweeping new full-fastback roofline patterned on that of Ford's Le Mans-winning GT40 racer. This brochure shot also shows the optional GT and Exterior Decor packages. The latter was identified by a ribbed back panel and a special hood with turn-signal indicator lights in twin "scoops." *This page:* Despite greater visual bulk, Mustang's '67 styling kept the original car's lithe, ready-for-action look. This GT/A (GT with automatic transmission) convertible is fitted with the 320-horse 390 big-block and accessorized with tilt deluxe steering wheel, AM/FM radio, cruise control, extended console, and SelectAire air conditioning. The GT Equipment Group was available on any '67 Mustang equipped with one of the available V-8s.

Meantime, Carroll Shelby convincingly one-upped Ford with his '67 GT-350, applying a new fiberglass nose with two high-beam headlamps dead-center in the grille, as well as a larger hood scoop, sculpted brake-cooling scoops on the sides, and two more scoops on the rear roof for interior ventilation. A modest "lip" spoiler appeared above wide taillight clusters purloined from Cougar. In all, a busy but arresting package. Thanks to customer feedback and the stock Mustang's added weight, Shelby made power steering and brakes "mandatory options" (you still paid extra, but couldn't get a car without them). Unique interior appointments included a racing steering wheel, additional gauges, and a functional roll bar with inertia-reel shoulder harnesses.

But there was more. Typical of the man, Shelby bypassed the 390 and used Ford's physically similar 428 V-8 to create a new GT-500 fastback that promptly outsold the small-block model two to one. The GT-350 itself

retained a 289 warmed to Shelby specs, but without steel-tube headers and straight-through mufflers. Actual power was thus lower despite an unchanged 290-hp rating.

Less muscle and weighty new fluff naturally hurt GT-350 performance. The GT-500 was predictably quicker, yet somehow disappointing. Carmakers were now understating power figures to avoid running afoul of insurance companies. Shelby's 428 was thus billed at 355 hp, but was closer to 400. *Car and Driver*, whose test car clocked 6.5 seconds 0–60 mph, said that while the 428 "isn't the Le Mans winner," the GT-500 "does with ease what the [GT-350] took brute force to accomplish." But *Road & Track*, which got 7.2 seconds in the same sprint, said the GT-500 "simply doesn't have anything sensational to offer...." Shelby's answer was an optional

427—which was the Le Mans engine and conservatively listed at 390 hp— but few were ordered.

Mustang sales skidded to 317,404 for model-year 1968. Higher prices were a factor. The ragtop now started at more than $2800, and a few options could run that above $4000, a lot in those days. The arrival of American Motors' Javelin and AMX ponycars didn't help. Neither did little-changed styling: just smaller simulated side scoops and an inset grille with no horizontal bar, which left the pony emblem and GT fog lamps "floating" in space. Jazzy "C-stripes" tracing the bodyside character lines were newly available with the GT package, which was much as before: dual exhausts with chrome-plated "quad" outlets, pop-open fuel cap, heavy-duty suspension (high-rate springs, shocks, and front sway bar), and F70–14

Both pages: This handsome 1967 GT/A coupe is finished in Burnt Amber paint and wears "spider-web" styled steel wheels, one of the few items continued from 1965-66. Vinyl-covered roofs like the one shown here added $74.36. The grille-mounted fog lights and cool dual twin exhaust tips were included in the GT package. The 289 V-8 could be had with 200 hp to start, 225 in mid-level form, or 271 in the top "Hi-Po" version. The coupe was by far the most popular of the three body styles, accounting for 356,271 of the 472,121 Mustangs sold in '67. The 2+2 was a distant second with 71,042, while only 44,808 convertibles were built.

This page: The center-mounted driving lights of the 1967 Shelby GT-350 didn't conform to local laws in some states; Shelby also offered units mounted at the outboard edges of the grille. Unlike regular Mustangs, the Shelby's lower side scoop was functional and channeled air to the rear brakes. The roof-pillar side scoop extracted air from the cabin. The GT-350 came with the small-block 289, which for '67 was a 306-horse "Cobra-ized" version of the solid-lifter Hi-Po 289. *Opposite page, top:* The 1967 Shelby GT-500s packed a 428-cid V-8 with two Holley four-barrel carbs, plus a unique oval-finned, open element air cleaner and cast aluminum valve covers. *Bottom:* Jerry Titus wheeled a Shelby-prepared Mustang coupe in the SCCA's 1967 Trans-Am series, scoring four wins and securing the manufacturer's title for Ford.

whitewall tires on six-inch-wide styled steel wheels. Aggressive Wide Oval tires were again sold separately.

Engine choices were more numerous than ever for '68. The base 200-cid six and two-barrel 289 V-8 each lost five hp to lower compression, this to meet new 50-state federal emissions standards, but the 390 was uprated to 335. A first-time optional six was added—a 250 lifted from Ford's truck line and offering 155 hp for just $26 extra—but four-speed manual was no longer available for any six-cylinder Mustang. The high-winding four-barrel 289 also departed, but its role as the middle V-8 was filled by a considerably changed small-block stroked out to 302 cid and a rated 230 hp. Topping the chart at a whopping $755 was Ford's mighty 427 big-block,

This page: While many '68 Mustangs were fitted with big-block V-8s, owners who were less interested in brute power discovered that the small-block eights, such as the optional 289 two-barrel in this Brittany Blue fastback, gave lively performance, thanks in large part to the relative light weight of the cars' front ends. (This would be the final year for the Mustang 289, which would be superseded by the 302 for 1969.) A peppy 195 horsepower, working through a three-speed stick, as on this car, made the driving experience all the more satisfying. The center console was a popular option. The heavily padded two-spoke steering wheel was a response to new safety regulations. *Opposite page, left:* Sold only for '68 in the Golden State, the "California Special" hardtop offered Shelby-Mustang style for much less money. Some 5000 were built. *Right:* This 1968 GT 2+2 sports bodyside "C-stripes" and new multi-hole styled steel wheels. All models exchanged a protruding grille for an inset piece without crossbars. The running-horse emblem "floated" in the cavity, as did the GT-standard outboard fog lamps.

with tight 10.9:1 compression and a conservative 390-hp rating. Though restricted to Cruise-O-Matic, it was good for 0–60-mph times of around six seconds, making for the fastest showroom-stock Mustang yet. But like the 390, it tended to overwhelm the front suspension, and that plus a formidable price limited sales. Mustang's optional power front-disc brakes switched from fixed to floating calipers, which provided extra stopping with no extra pedal effort. Wisely, Ford made front discs mandatory for 390 and 427 models.

The 427 was hastily retired at midyear and replaced by the 428 Cobra Jet, a huskier version of the super-torquey low-revving big-block lately offered in Thunderbirds and big Fords. For drag racing and insurance purposes, it was advertised at 335 hp on 10.7:1 compression but was undoubtedly much stronger.

Lengthening Mustang's '68 option roster was a Sports Trim Group with woodgrain dash, two-tone hood paint (also available separately), "Comfort-Weave" vinyl seat inserts, wheel lip moldings on six-cylinder models, and fatter tires on styled steel wheels for V-8 cars. Other new extras included a rear-window defogger and Fingertip Speed Control. A spring/summer

Sprint package offered V-8 power, bodyside C-stripes, pop-open gas cap, and full wheel covers or Wide Oval tires on styled wheels.

Shelby Mustangs for 1968 got a few visual updates: a full-width hood scoop, hood louvers, a larger grille with square running lamps (not driving lights), sequential rear turn signals, and miscellaneous trim shuffles. More significant were Shelby's first convertibles, a GT-350 and GT-500 with a built-in rollover hoop. Luxury options like air conditioning, tilt steering wheel, tinted glass, and AM/FM stereo now outnumbered performance features.

Indeed, federal emissions standards prompted switching the GT-350 to Ford's new 302 V-8. Rated hp sank to 250, down 40. A Paxton supercharger option, revived from '66, added about 100 horses, but again found few takers. Among big-block '68 Shelbys, GT-500s retained the previous 428, albeit re-rated to 360 hp, but the engine was in short supply due to a plant strike, so some cars got ordinary 390s. Buyers weren't told of the substitution, and it was nearly impossible to spot. Mid-model year brought some redress in the replacement GT-500KR—"King of the Road." Also offered in fastback and convertible form, it carried a new Cobra Jet 428,

Opposite page: Ford built 52 special Cobra Jet fastbacks in December 1967 to homologate the car for Super Stock drag racing. The menacing 428 Cobra Jet V-8 was conservatively rated at 335 hp, and it instantly made the Mustang a real dragstrip threat. Factory-backed drag racer "Dyno" Don Nicholson was one of the most popular (and successful) Cobra-Jet Mustang pilots. *Right:* Sequential taillights picked up from the 1965 T-Bird were the most noticeable change at the rear of this year's Shelbys. In 1968, Ford shifted Shelby production from Carroll Shelby's Los Angeles plant to Livonia, Michigan (not far from Dearborn), where contractor A. O. Smith carried out the conversions. *This page, below:* The 1968 Shelby Cobra GT-500 fastback carried a steep-for-the-day sticker price of $4317. All '68 Shelby Mustangs got a revised nose with a larger, more-aggressive grille opening. As before, hood and bodyside scoops were functional, as were those of the fastback roof. Interiors, though, were becoming as plush as those in any regular Mustang.

basically the existing mill with big-port 427 heads, larger intake manifold and exhaust system, and an estimated 40 extra horses. Shelby also tossed in wider rear brakes.

Like other American cars, the 1968 Mustangs gained new safety features per government decree. Heading the list were an energy-absorbing steering column, retracting seatbelts, standard backup lights, dual-circuit brake system, hazard warning flashers, side-marker lights, and energy-absorbing seatbacks.

Mustang's second consecutive sales decline caused understandable concern among some FoMoCo executives, who began to wonder if the car was losing its appeal. To be sure, the advent of rival ponycars had stolen Mustang's thunder, but the real problem was that buyer interest in the ponycar itself was starting to wane barely four years after Ford had pioneered the market.

Of course, nobody could know this at the time. For the moment, "more is better" remained an article of faith in Detroit, as the next Mustang would most certainly show.

3

Mustang had more of everything for 1969—except more buyers. And 1970 sales were lower still. Was Mustang losing its magic? The question was particularly important to a new company president, recruited from a surprising source, who immediately made his mark with two of the greatest cars in performance history.

1969–1970: A STEED FOR EVERY NEED

The 1969 Mustangs premiered soon after veteran General Motors executive Semon E. "Bunkie" Knudsen was named Ford Motor Company president. It was the most startling defection Detroit had seen since the 1920s, when Bunkie's father, William S. Knudsen, left Ford for Chevrolet. Bunkie brought along talented Larry Shinoda to head up Ford's Special Design Center, but both arrived too late to influence '69 Mustang development.

That work got underway in October 1965. Curious first thoughts of a mini-Thunderbird soon gave way to a husky muscle-car-type package that was ultimately toned down. Even so, the '69s ended up four inches longer than the 1967–68 models. They were also slightly lower, wider, and heavier (the last betrayed by a larger fuel tank). Wheelbase remained at 108 inches, but front shoulder room and rear legroom each improved by 2.5 inches. Outside, Mustang's familiar face gained an extra pair of headlights

within the grille, the old side sculpturing was erased, rear fenders bulged more noticeably, and the back panel was now concave.

Two models were added. An upscale Grandé hardtop offered a vinyl roof, wire wheel covers, and bodyside pinstripes, plus imitation teak interior trim and some 55 extra pounds of sound insulation, for $2866, some $230 more than the standard issue. More exciting was the Mach 1 fastback. A $3139 intruder into Shelby territory, it sported simulated rear-quarter air ducts, a decklid spoiler, and a functional "Shaker" hood scoop that stuck up from the air cleaner through a hole in the hood, where it vibrated madly. With that plus sweeping "SportsRoof" styling, the Mach 1 looked every inch a performance machine. And with a standard 351-cubic-inch V-8 producing 250 horsepower, it was.

The 351 was devised to plug a displacement gap in Ford's engine lineup. Descended from the original 260 small-block of 1962, it was basically a 302

Chapter 3: 1969-1970 | **43**

with a half-inch-longer stroke. We're speaking here of the 351 "Windsor" engine, not the equally famous "Cleveland" unit. Both were named for their factories, but the Canadian-built Windsor started production in autumn 1968, a year ahead of the Cleveland. Despite many premium features, the Windsor would play low-tune "economy V-8" in most Dearborn models. The Cleveland was designed for performance, with a unique block and an integral timing-chain chamber and water-crossover passage. It had a one-inch-higher deck versus the 302 and differed from the Windsor in having canted valves, wedge-shape combustion chambers, and shorter port areas giving more-direct gas flow.

Other Mustang engines were much as before. The 200- and optional 250-cid sixes gained no horsepower, but ran more smoothly on new "center percussion" mounts. The base 302 V-8 dropped 10 hp to 220, but was little changed otherwise. The Mach 1's 351 Windsor was optional for lesser Mustangs. So was a 290-hp Cleveland and—making a last stand— the old reliable 320-hp 390. The beefy 428 Cobra Jet returned with and without Ram-Air induction and a conservative 335-hp rating in each case. Included with the CJ option was a heavy-duty suspension with staggered rear shocks—one ahead of the rear axle, the other behind—to reduce wheel tramp in hard takeoffs.

New excitement arrived in early 1969 with the Boss 302 fastback, conceived to beat the Camaro Z-28 in the Sports Car Club of America's Trans-American road-racing series for ponycars and compact sedans. (It might have been called Trans-Am had Pontiac not grabbed the name for its hottest '69 Firebird.) Ford had to make 1000 to qualify the Boss 302 as "production," but ended up turning out 1934 of the '69s. Street versions were easy to spot with their matte-black rear-window slats a la Lamborghini's Miura, plus an adjustable rear airfoil and a four-inch-deep front air dam, all courtesy of Shinoda. The aero aids proved highly effective on the track. So did a special high-output (HO) engine that was (under-) rated at 290 hp. Features included big-port "Cleveland" heads, solid lifters, lightweight pistons, aluminum high-riser manifold, Holley four-barrel carb,

Opposite page, top: Design work toward the '69 Mustang began in October 1965. Efforts immediately focused on much greater size and luxury-car styling cues. Ford managers encouraged this direction in early '66 by ordering "more Thunderbird influence" be worked in. Typical of the results was this hardtop workout with an extended hood, large "loop" bumper/grille, upswept beltline, and thick rear roof quarters. *Middle and bottom:* This pair of mockups from mid-1966 show just a few of the many ideas rejected for '69, including swoopier "sweepspear" treatments and a more formal, Mercury Cougar-esque profile. *This page, top:* Though recognizably Mustang, the '69s were markedly different in size and appearance. Renamed "SportsRoof," the '69 fastback looked faster even in the standard trim shown here. *Right:* The new-for-'69 Grandé was a $2866 upscale hardtop with standard vinyl roof, wire wheel covers, special cloth/vinyl upholstery, and convincing faux teakwood interior trim.

This page: The Grandé effectively delivered a classier vibe than other Mustangs, thanks in part to an extra helping of sound-deadening insulation. Grandé sales topped 22,000 units this year. *Opposite page:* Mustang's other mainstream new-comer for '69, the $3139 Mach 1 fastback embodied youthful high per-formance and thus got most of the year's advertising emphasis. Ford's new 351 V-8 was standard, but the potent Cobra Jet was optional. So was a novel "shaker" hood scoop.

dual-point ignition, four-bolt central main-bearing caps, forged crank, and an ignition cut-out to prevent accidental over-revving. The Boss 302 also came with ultra-stiff springs, staggered shocks, a 4-speed gearbox pulling a shortish final drive (Detroit "Locker" differentials were available), heavy-duty brakes with 11.3-inch-diameter front discs, and F60-15 Polyglas tires in radiused wheelarches. A Traction-Lok limited-slip diff was optional, as were Autolite "inline" four-barrel carbs on a "Cross Boss" manifold.

A genuine surprise was the Boss 429, a brutish big-block fastback born of Ford's desire to run its new "semi-hemi" 429 V-8 in NASCAR. Rules mandated 500 production installations but didn't specify models. Though Torino was the Blue Oval's stock-car weapon, Ford decided to put street 429s in a Mustang. Besides "crescent-shaped" combustion chambers, the engine employed a thin-wall block, aluminum heads, beefed-up main bearings, and a cross-drilled steel-billeted crank. There were actually two versions of this "820" powerplant: a hydraulic-lifter "S" unit fitted to the first 279 cars, and a later "T" edition with different rods and pistons and mechanical or hydraulic lifters. Both were rated at 360 hp in street form or

375 hp in race trim, but—as with the HO 302—those were lowball numbers to placate insurance companies.

Because this was another highly specialized limited edition, Ford assigned Boss 429 production to Kar Kraft, a low-volume constructor in Brighton, Michigan. Installing the extra-wide engine required altering front suspension and inner fender wells, adding diagonal braces between wheelhouses and firewall (to resist body twist from the engine's massive torque), and moving the battery to the trunk (no room for it up front). For good measure, tracks were widened and wheel arches flared to accommodate F60-15 tires on seven-inch-wide Magnum 500 wheels. Also standard were an engine oil cooler, power steering and brakes, and a Traction-Lok limited-slip differential. (A Detroit No-Spin axle was optional.) Oddly perhaps, the 429 was more visually subtle than its little brother or the Mach 1: just ID decals, a Boss 302-style rear wing, plus a specific front airdam and working hood scoop. It was also surprisingly lush for a factory drag racer. Each one had the Decor Group that was optional on everyday Mustangs, plus high-back front seats, a center console, and woodgrain dash trim. Ford even threw in the optional Visibility Group with lights for trunk, ashtray, and glovebox. Automatic transmission and air conditioning weren't available, but the big Boss was the costliest non-Shelby Mustang to date at $4798.

Not that either Boss was intended to make money. They were "homologation specials" built to satisfy racing rules. *Car Life* tested both and found the little guy quicker to 60 mph—6.9 seconds versus 7.2—though it lost in the quarter-mile at 14.85 seconds/96.14 mph versus 14.09/102.85. Reported top speed was 118 mph in each case. But though the Boss 429 was fearsome when modified for the strip, its chassis was so easily overwhelmed in hard acceleration that the street version was almost a disappointment. Not so the Boss 302, which in *Car Life*'s tests turned the exact same quarter-mile time as Camaro's Z-28. "It's what the Shelby [GTs] should have been but weren't," enthused *Car and Driver*, all of which made for a peerless performance buy even at a not-inexpensive $3588.

Opposite page: Ford stepped up its SCCA Trans-Am racing efforts for 1969 with specially prepared Boss 302 Mustangs. *This page:* Ford introduced two Boss Mustangs as limited-production midyear specials. Both were primarily for homologation purposes: The flashy Boss 302 was for SCCA racing, and the more sedately trimmed Boss 429 was built so Ford could use its fearsome "semi-hemi" Boss 429 engine in NASCAR competition.

This page: The Boss 429 mill was so large that the Mustang engine bay needed substantial modifications—including wider spring towers, shorter upper control arms, and staggered shocks—for it to fit. Despite the exotic powerplant underhood, the Boss 429 was unusually understated; a hood scoop, front chin spoiler, and subtle front-fender decals were its only special exterior details. *Opposite page:* Carroll Shelby flashes the usual Texas-size grin in posing with three of "his" Mustangs for 1969. Actually, the cars were conceived and built entirely by Ford. These were the tamest Shelbys yet, but a GT-500 like the Grabber Blue convertible shown here could still turn heads—and race through the 0–60 sprint in under six seconds.

C/D's reference was telling, because the '69 Shelbys were Ford's work, not Carroll's—little more than a custom styling job on the new fastback and convertible. GT-350 and GT-500 versions of each returned with a fiberglass nose and a big loop bumper/grille that added three inches to overall length versus stock. Scoops sprouted everywhere, and wide reflective tape stripes ran midway along the flanks. Despite this visual brag, added weight and stiffening emission controls made these the tamest Shelbys ever. The GT-500 retained that '68 KR's 335-hp 428 CJ engine, but lost 25 horses by most estimates. The GT-350 graduated to the 351 Windsor, but advertised power was 290, same as the previous 302—and the Mach 1 offered the same engine for much less money.

Thanks to the combination of less performance and new intramural competition, Shelby production plunged 25 percent for 1969 to 3150 units. After seeing his car win only one Trans-Am race in 1969, Ol' Shel retired from the car business, though not forever, as we know, and not before convincing Ford to end the Shelby-Mustang program. Before the hammer

fell, a little over 600 unsold '69s were made into "1970" models with Boss 302 front spoilers, black hoods, and new serial numbers.

Mustang itself had more competition for 1970, with Dodge's belated Challenger and a completely redone Plymouth Barracuda followed at midyear by a handsome new second-series Chevy Camaro/Pontiac Firebird. Little wonder that model-year volume suffered another big hit, dropping from 299,821 units to 190,727. This partly reflected the fast-withering demand for ponycars in general, but also a relative lack of change. All seven Mustang models returned with a mild but tasteful facelift featuring dual headlamps and a flat-again back panel. Mechanicals changed little. New appearance options for fastbacks included Boss-type backlight louvers, an adjustable rear spoiler, and bodyside C-stripes. An optional

Opposite page, top: Among 1970 Ford concept cars was the vividly violet Mustang Milano with a Shelby-esque schnoz, a chopped top with flowing lines a la big brother Torino, and a predictive rear liftgate. *Opposite page, bottom:* Production Mustang styling was visibly cleaner for 1970, especially on standard-trim models like this convertible. Highlights included the return of dual headlamps in a new thin-bar grille, tinsel-free bodysides, and recessed headlamps. *This page:* For its second season, the Mach 1 was given ribbed lower body panels, a boldly striped hood, and grille-mounted driving lights. Like other 1970 fastbacks, the Mach 1 lost its upper-bodyside scoops but gained the Boss 302's rear-window louvers as a new option.

This page: The Boss 302 returned for one more year with "hockey-stick" tape striping, an optional "shaker" hood scoop, and the same high-profile appeal. This unusually trimmed prototype wears Magnum 500 wheels with argent-finished centers; production versions had chrome centers with the depressed areas finished in black. Sad to say, Ford bailed out from all forms of racing after 1970, Trans-Am included, so the Boss 302 would not return for a third season. *Opposite page, top:* Like its small-block brother, the Boss 429 would not return after 1970. In this case though, the reason had less to do with Ford's decision to leave racing than with falling demand for performance cars in general, aggravated by period price inflation and inflating insurance premiums. *Bottom:* The Shelby GTs reached the end of their road in 1970 after Carroll Shelby decided to cease being a car manufacturer and asked Ford to end these once-special Mustangs. Some 600 leftover '69s were reserialed as "1970" models and given black hood striping and Boss 302 airdams, as shown on this GT-500 coupe.

Hurst shift linkage was also new. Mach 1 again wore its own grille, now with built-in driving lamps. It still came with the GT Equipment Group, but that package was no longer offered for other models, though they were treated to standard Mach 1-style high-back bucket seats.

Prices hadn't climbed much since the early days. The basic six-cylinder hardtop still listed at only a bit over $2700, the V-8 convertible for as little as $3126. Alas, only about 7700 Mustang ragtops were built for 1970, reflecting a general market shift away from convertibles.

Another 6319 Boss 302s were built, and they would be the last, as the car was no longer needed once Ford withdrew from Trans-Am racing after claiming the 1970 championship. (Camaro Z-28s had prevailed in 1968–69.) The Boss 429 also departed after a final 505 copies, all built during '69.

Despite the worrisome trends in ponycar sales, Ford had big plans for '71—literally. Bunkie was about to have his day with a Mustang unlike any seen before.

An all-new Mustang galloped in for 1971, when
buyers were moving on and the ponycar market
was shrinking fast. But despite the bad timing and
a herd of challenging new federal regulations,
Mustang still offered high style and—with the right
options—great performance.

1971–1973: BIG EVENTS

Bunkie Knudsen lasted less than two years as Ford Motor Company president, but that was long enough to leave his mark on the 1971 Mustang. Chairman Henry Ford II replaced Knudsen with a presidential triumvirate that included Lee Iacocca. A year later, in late 1970, he made Iacocca overall president, in part as a reward for "fathering" the Mustang. But Iacocca had little to do with the '71, having been Ford Division general manager since 1965, a job that entailed no direct product-development responsibility.

Work on the '71 Mustangs was underway by May 1967, about nine months before Knudsen arrived in Dearborn. Most initial clay models looked heavy and Thunderbird-ish to the point of clumsiness. Designers eventually stripped away the flab, opting for crisp, severely creased lines married to bulging fenders and kicked-up "ducktails." The overall design and package size were settled by September 1968 and had Knudsen's blessing.

The result was the biggest Mustang ever: eight inches longer than the 1969–70 models, six inches wider, and some 600 pounds heavier on a new 109-inch wheelbase. The trademark long hood/short deck proportions were retained, but styling was more flamboyant than ever, reflecting the tastes of Knudsen and designer Larry Shinoda (who departed Dearborn when Bunkie did). Most noticeable were an almost horizontal fastback roofline, a blunted nose, and a more acutely angled windshield with hidden wipers. The last betrayed Shinoda's GM background, as did a new reverse-slant dashboard.

While all this made sense in the late '60s, it did not fit the much-changed market and regulatory landscape of model-year '71, when total ponycar sales were half of what they'd been in best-ever 1967. Buyers were now flocking to compact cars like Ford's own Pinto and Maverick in the face of soaring insurance premiums on "hot cars" and cars that simply looked hot.

Detroit performance was also threatened by a raft of new government-mandated emissions standards that took effect within days of Iacocca's becoming Ford president. These required ever-steeper reductions of hydrocarbon (HC), carbon monoxide (CO), and oxides of nitrogen (NOx) that would only be achieved with the post-1974 adoption of the catalytic converter, a sort of "afterburner" that either neutralized noxious gases or formed less harmful ones (such as changing CO to carbon dioxide).

More immediately, General Motors cut compression on its 1971 car engines to accommodate low-lead and no-lead gasoline, then coming on the scene to help meet emissions targets. Ford, Chrysler, and American Motors followed suit for '72. In a related move, all U.S. makers except Ford quoted two sets of horsepower figures for '71: traditional SAE gross (dynamometer readings of engines without fan drive, exhaust system, or other accessories), and more realistic SAE net figures (with ancillaries installed as in an actual car). Dearborn grudgingly joined in for '72.

Engineers also scrambled to meet a new requirement for bumpers that could absorb five-mph shunts without damage to headlights or other "safety-related equipment." These would be required at the front on '73 models and at both ends on '74 and later models. Given existing technology, "crash bumpers" meant extra weight that hurt fuel economy, though that caused little concern at a time when gas was still plentiful and cheap (50 cents a gallon).

The advent of color-keyed polyurethane bumper covers enabled the '71 Mach 1 to meet the crash-bumper edict with style. It also received twin dummy hood scoops (optional on other models) and a specific grille with a small running horse on honeycomb mesh, flanked by horizontal parking lamps. Other Mustang grilles retained the traditional large, chrome-framed horse and revived a horizontal divider bar.

Most Mustang engines were detuned for 1971. The 200-cubic-inch six was dropped—sensible in light of the weight gain—and the 250 lost 10 horsepower, settling for 145. Among V-8s, the base two-barrel 302 also dropped 10 horses, to 210. So did the two-barrel 351, now at 240 hp;

Opposite page: In January 1968, new Ford president Bunkie Knudsen chose a fastback mockup as the basis for '71 Mustang styling. It was quickly refined with an eye to manufacturing cost and feasibility. These workouts, from September 1968, show various thoughts on body details such as scoops and sculpture lines. *This page, top left:* The hardtop '71 Mustang was also taking shape in September 1968, when this mockup was photographed in the Ford Design Center courtyard. *Top right:* A convertible mockup from early 1969 is very close to the '71 ragtop that greeted buyers in Ford showrooms, but the taillights would be tweaked. As usual, designers debated such details almost until the last minute. *Bottom:* When this '71 standard fastback Mustang went on sale, Bunkie was gone, but his influence on Mustang styling would last through '73.

This page: Mach 1 looked meaner than ever for '71 but packed less standard power, demoted from a 351 V-8 to a mild 302. This one, however, has the big 429 Cobra Jet V-8. *Opposite page:* A new body-colored front bumper and honeycomb grille dressed up the front end of the '71 Mach 1. *Car Life* magazine called Mustang's fastback a "flat back" because the rear window was pitched only 14 degrees from horizontal. It looked racy but played hob with visibility.

a four-barrel version returned with 285. New to the mix was the Boss 351 Cleveland with four-barrel carburetor and 330 gross hp. Despite high 11.0:1 compression, it was more tractable than the departed HO 302 and more durable, as it wasn't as high-revving. Also new was a four-barrel 429 Cobra Jet that replaced the 428 CJ to deliver 370 hp with or without Ram Air induction. There was also a Super Cobra Jet boasting 375 hp.

Though still a high-performer in standard trim, the Mach 1 could again be ordered with air conditioning ($407), automatic transmission ($238), and conveniences like tilt steering wheel and a "sport deck" rear seat (a fold-

down job as offered on fastback Mustangs since '65). Also available were a sports interior ($130), power front-disc brakes ($70), center console ($60), and instrument group ($54). Liberal use of the option book could raise the $3268 base price to well over $5500. No-cost items again included high-back bucket seats, front spoiler, dual exhausts, and racing-style door mirrors.

The 429 CJ option cost $436 but paid dividends for Mach 1 performance: 0–60 mph in 6.5 seconds, the standing quarter-mile in 14.5. Top speed was about 115 mph with automatic and 3.25:1 rear axle, fuel

This page: Though less fiery than the Boss models it replaced, the Boss 351 fastback was the quickest, most roadable '71 in the Mustang stable. A special High-Output 351 V-8 with premium internals delivered a solid 330 hp through a four-speed manual gearbox with Hurst shifter, good for 0–60 in under six seconds. Alas, hot-car demand was waning fast, and Ford fired the Boss at midseason after building only 1800. *Opposite page:* The Boss 351 shared a NACA-scooped hood secured by twist-lock hood pins with the Mach 1. The sticker price of $4124 was steep by 1971 standards and helped limit sales.

"economy" 10–11 mpg. "It is a decent mixture for those who want good performance and some comfort," said *Motor Trend*, "but it still remains a little unwieldy for city traffic."

The Boss 351 V-8 powered a new like-named fastback filling the "racer's Mustang" role. It looked much like the Mach 1 save name decals, mid-flank striping, and a Boss-type front spoiler. *MT* tested this one too, and found it handled better than the Mach 1, thanks to uprated front-coil springs, staggered and stiffer rear shocks, and hefty front/rear stabilizer bars. The Boss 351 also proved quicker, clocking 0–60 in 5.8 seconds and the quarter-mile in 13.8, though a short 3.91:1 rear axle limited top speed to about 100 mph.

Against these potent V-8s, the base 302 was pretty tame. It typically delivered 10-second 0–60s and 17.5-second quarter-miles (with 2.79:1 axle and automatic). Yet this was decent performance by 1971 standards, as was mileage (up to 17 mpg).

This page: Styling changes were few for '72. Chrome wheel-lip and rocker trim was now standard (vs. optional) on Mustangs, but this early promotional photo of a base hardtop lacks that trim. *Opposite page:* The new Sprint Decor Option was available for hardtops, fastbacks, and convertibles. The option came two ways: A basic "A" package comprised white paint with color-matched plastic-covered front bumper; broad blue hood stripes, rocker panels, and rear-end accents edged in red; racing mirrors; wheel trim rings; and "U.S.A" flag decals on the rear fenders. Interiors were color-coordinated in vinyl with blue cloth inserts for the seats. A second package bundled all this with Magnum 500 wheels, F60-15 white-letter tires, and firm competition suspension. Total Sprint orders apparently weren't tallied, but were probably low. It is known that Ford built just 50 Sprint convertibles.

Overall, the '71 Mustangs were not bad cars, but they weren't especially great, either. So despite the redesign, sales kept sliding, with model-year production of 149,678 units. That included an estimated 1800 copies of the Boss 351, which was dumped at mid-season.

Even stricter emissions limits dictated further engine detuning for 1972, and the big 429, one reason for the '71's greater size, was eliminated. As mentioned, Ford now joined other Detroit automakers in quoting net horsepower. The 250 six was thus more accurately advertised at 95 hp, the 302 at 136 hp, and 351s at 168/200/275 hp. The last figure applied to a revised Boss 351 called 351 HO, a late addition to the option chart.

But little else changed, leaving Ford to talk mostly of new colors and fabrics. Among these was a Sprint Decor Option delivering white paint set off by broad blue patches on hood, lower body, and back panel, plus large American-flag decals on the rear fenders. "Control and balance make it a beautiful experience," said the ads, but 1972 Mustang sales looked none too beautiful to Ford accountants, who tallied another dip to 125,093 units, off about 20 percent.

Sales recovered to 135,267 for '73, even though the big steeds were again little changed. The ragtop scored the largest increase—a resounding 100 percent to nearly 2000 units. But that was mainly because Ford had

Chapter 4: 1971–1973 | **65**

announced that the body style would not return, the result of a pending government mandate for rollover protection that, ironically, was never enacted. It would be a decade before Ford got back to factory-built Mustang convertibles.

Apart from surprisingly unobtrusive five-mph front bumpers, the '73 Mustangs were visual reruns. As before, Mach 1 nose styling was available for other models in an Exterior Decor Group, albeit with the "sport" parking lamps turned from horizontal to vertical. Prices were little changed from '72, when they'd been cut to spark sales. The base six-cylinder hardtop listed at $2760, while the V-8 convertible topped the line at $3189. The Grandé hardtop, still hanging in with standard 302 and posh appointments, stickered at $3088—down $124 from '71. The '73 Mach 1,

Opposite page: As performance waned in the 70s, the luxury-themed Grandé model gained importance. By 1973, Grandé production set a record with 25,274 units, or 18.7 percent of the total Mustang production run—up from 7.4 percent in debut-year 1969. A full vinyl top was standard on Grandés such as this Medium Brown 1973 model. *This page:* For 1973, all Mustangs wore a color-keyed front bumper that was redesigned to meet the government's "five-mph" impact standard, taking effect that year. Parking lights moved up to the grille from under the bumper. A grille insert with enlarged eggcrates further freshened the Grandé hardtop (shown) and base models. The Grandé interior was still quite plush considering the model's $2946 base price.

again with standard two-barrel 351, also started at $3088. Options were as plentiful as ever: vinyl top, forged-aluminum wheels, "metallic glow" paint, decorative side stripes, raised-white-letter tires, firm "competition suspension," and a useful new electric rear-window defroster for closed models.

Technical updates began with bigger brakes, factory-optional radial tires, and an available "dual ram induction" hood for cars with the two-barrel 351. The last featured working twin air scoops, matte black or silver paint, and twist-type hood locks, all borrowed from the Mach 1. A two-tone hood with dummy scoops was available with the 302. Mustang was now the only Ford offering the HO 351. As elsewhere in Detroit, drivetrain choices were thinning due to the high cost of certifying each permutation for emissions

This page: Though most engines lost a few more horses for '73, Mustang could still be dressed to thrill. This convertible sports two options offered that year: polished aluminum wheels and Mach-style twin-scoop hood. A useful Instrumentation Group was still available. The '73 convertible would be Mustang's last until 1983. *Opposite page:* New bodyside striping and a bolder honeycomb texture on the back panel, hood scoops, and grille were the main visual differences unique to the '73 Mach 1. Though 1971–73 Mustangs are often criticized for excessive nose-plowing understeer, especially in tight corners, sportier models like the Mach 1 could be reasonably agile for their size and heft.

compliance under the EPA's newly mandated 50,000-mile durability test. All engines adopted crankcase ventilation and exhaust-gas recirculation. The latter routed gases from the exhaust manifold through a vacuum valve into the carburetor to be diluted by the incoming fuel/air mixture. This permitted leaner carburetor settings for lower emissions.

More new federal edicts were evident inside. The dash got extra padding and was shorn of projections that might cause injury in a crash. Less welcome was a "starter interlock" that prevented ignition if a front occupant didn't buckle up. Though mandated for all 1972 cars, this device proved so irksome that Washington rescinded the requirement after model-year '73.

The 1971–73 models would be the last Mustangs descended directly from the smash-hit mid-'60s original. But though the winning traits of sporty styling, brisk-to-vivid performance, and a long option list had been preserved, everyone knew that Ford had veered too far from the ponycar idea and needed to get back on track. Dearborn was about to do just that with a much smaller Mustang for the ever-more challenging world of the Seventies. Unfortunately, the new colt would prove no less controversial than the "Clydesdales" it replaced.

With Lee Iacocca back in the saddle, Ford's ponycar revisited its roots. A dramatically smaller, lighter design marked a fresh start, and the new Mustang II couldn't have been better timed for the market climate of the day.

1974-1978: STARTING OVER

If nothing else, the Mustang II deserves credit for keeping Ford's ponycar alive through a difficult period for all Detroit. It was accidentally well timed, bowing on the eve of the 1973-74 Energy Crisis that surely spurred interest in a smaller, more fuel-efficient ponycar. After all, first-year sales were a smashing 385,993, just 10 percent shy of the '65 Mustang's record 418,812.

Impetus for the Mustang II came from the steady decline in ponycar sales after 1967 and from the growing popularity of sporty imports like the Toyota Celica and Ford's own British/German Capri. While such "mini-ponycars" sold fewer than 100,000 units in 1965, they did 300,000 in '72 and were forecast to top 400,000 by '74.

Ford president Lee Iacocca took note of this and ordered a series of consumer clinics to gauge prospects for a sporty new domestic compact Ford. Though response was favorable, development lagged until Iacocca sought ideas from Italian coachbuilder Ghia, which Ford took over in late

1970. Ghia submitted a sloped-nose fastback prototype that Iacocca took as the starting point for an intramural design contest of the sort he'd used on the original Mustang. Begun in August 1971, it involved the Ford and Lincoln-Mercury divisional studios, Advanced Design, and the Interior Studio. Iacocca dictated a 96-100-inch wheelbase; pillared notchback and/or fastback coupe body styles; available four-speed manual gearbox; and a four-cylinder or small six-cylinder engine. Most important, the car "must be luxurious...and carefully built"—in short, "a little jewel."

Management reviewed five full-size clay models in late November 1971 and chose a fastback from the L-M team. The design was little altered for production, but not all executives liked it—or the derivative notchback. Actually, the notch wasn't approved until a bare 16 months before production start-up, saved only by positive reaction at one last consumer clinic. At least the fastback was more practical than earlier "SportsRoof"

models by dint of a European-style rear hatch "door," a first for a Mustang. A two-seat fastback was also proposed, but never seriously considered.

The Mustang II continued its predecessors' long-hood/short-deck proportions, but on a reduced scale—smaller than even the original. Against the '73 Mustang, it was a whopping 20 inches shorter, nearly 13 inches shorter in wheelbase, four inches narrower, and a significant 400–500 pounds lighter. The interior, developed by a group under veteran Ford designer L. David Ash, featured an instrument panel far more sensible than recent Mustang dashboards. A large oblong design put all controls ahead of the driver, along with easy-read gauges including a standard tachometer. Seats were initially covered in pleated cloth, vinyl, or optional leather.

Some suggested the Mustang II was just a sportier version of the 1971–73 subcompact Pinto. But though Ford grudgingly admitted that many components were shared, there were many differences too. For example, both cars used the same double-A-arm front suspension, but the Mustang's attached to a rubber-mounted subframe instead of the main structure. This reduced driveline vibration into the cabin and contributed to more precise steering and a smoother ride. Mustang II also boasted longer rear leaf springs, staggered shocks, and damping computer-matched to model and weight. The luxury Ghia notchback, for example, got softish settings, while the optional competition suspension had the stiffest springs and a thicker front anti-roll bar.

Iacocca's final design brief did not mention a V-8, another first for a Mustang—and no bulky inline six. Initial engine choices thus boiled down to a 2.3-liter (140-cubic-inch) single-overhead-cam inline four-cylinder and a 2.8-liter (171-cid) enlargement of the Capri's overhead-valve V-6. The "Lima" four-cylinder (named for the Lima, Ohio, plant that built it) was basically a larger version of the Pinto's 2.0-liter engine. The V-6 was changed from siamesed to separate exhaust ports for better performance and thermal efficiency. It was standard in a new Mach 1 hatchback, optional otherwise. The manual gearbox was basically a beefed-up Pinto four-speed, while the optional automatic transmission was a modified three-speed Cruise-O-

Opposite page, top: Italian coachbuilder Ghia submitted two prototypes that helped focus Ford designers. This later model revived Mustang's original bodyside sculpturing. *Middle and bottom:* A notchback body style wasn't initially in the cards, but this nicely proportioned prototype helped change Ford executives' minds. *This page, top left:* The crisp edges of the notchback prototype got "softer" in the path to production. *Middle left:* This September 1971 fastback model wasn't Ghia's but did show Italian influence. *Above:* Just like old times: Lee Iacocca poses with the new Mustang II and its nearly ten-year-old precursor on August 28, 1973. *Left:* Mustang II coupes came in base or fancier Ghia trim (shown here). Whitewall radial tires, a vinyl roof with Ghia badge, and vinyl bodyside molding were just a few of the Ghia's distinguishing features.

Matic. Standard vacuum-assist brakes comprised 9.3-inch front discs and 9 x 1.75-inch rear drums.

Not surprisingly, Mustang IIs exhibited "American" ride and handling characteristics. And because they were heavy for their size—2650 to 2900 pounds at the curb—a manual V-6 model took a lengthy 13–14 seconds to run 0–60 mph. As if to prepare buyers for this reduced performance, Ford redesigned Mustang's trademark running-horse emblem as a less-muscular steed that seemed to be trotting instead of galloping. That symbolism went largely unnoticed, but not the car itself, as its terrific first-year sales attested.

The Mustang II would run five years without major change. Four-cylinder and V-6 notchback and fastback, luxury Ghia notchback (replacing the Grandé hardtop), and the Mach 1 fastback were cataloged throughout. All offered numerous options per Mustang tradition. Aside from air conditioning and various sound systems, the '74 roster included a vinyl top for notchbacks, a tilt/takeout sunroof, and forged-aluminum wheels.

The big news for 1975 was an optional V-8, the trusty 302 returning with 122 net horsepower, then 139 hp. Cooling requirements dictated larger grille eggcrates, a change applied to all models from here on. Ghia options expanded to include a flip-up glass "moonroof" and a Silver Luxury

Opposite page: Mustang II styling came from a fastback theme model by the Lincoln-Mercury studio, which was little altered for production. A "mouthy" grille, C-shaped side sculpting, and other elements linked the new mini-ponycar to the 1965 original. Bumpers were now body color front and rear. *This page, top:* The Mach 1 included sporty touches such as a standard V-6 engine, raised-white-letter radial tires, and black accent paint on the lower body and rear panel. At $3674 to start, it was the most expensive 1974 Mustang and also the rarest, with 44,046 produced. *Right:* As the Seventies progressed, "spring special" appearance packages became more and more prevalent as manufacturers sought to add showroom interest to existing models. This two-tone special paint edition Mustang debuted in mid-1975.

Package with Cranberry-color velour upholstery, silver paint, vinyl top, and a pretentious standup hood ornament. At the same time, the Ghia's rear-quarter glass was narrowed into "opera" windows, another period styling fad. Also new was an optional "extended-range" (17-gallon) fuel tank, betraying the fact that even small Fords could be rather thirsty. Mileage improved somewhat with adoption of the catalytic converter, heralded by midseason "MPG" models.

Despite the V-8 and other updates, Mustang II model-year volume dropped more than 50 percent for 1975 to 188,575. New competition—like Chevrolet's Vega-based Monza 2+2—was a factor in that and in a further slide to 187,567 for 1976. Familiarity then took a toll, the little-changed '77s tallying 153,173 orders.

Flashy fastback trim options highlighted 1976 developments. Straining to emulate the late, great Shelby Mustangs was a new Cobra II package comprising sports steering wheel, brushed-aluminum interior trim, a black-finish grille, styled steel wheels, louvered flip-out rear-quarter windows, front air dam, rear spoiler, and simulated hood air scoop, plus bold ID all over and radial tires. White paint contrasted with blue tape stripes in the usual places. Other color combinations were added for '77. The equally brash Stallion package featured snorting-horse-head decals and forged-aluminum wheels.

Options were again the main order of business for 1977. Ghias added a Sports Appearance Group with black or tan paint, color-keyed console, sport steering wheel, cast-aluminum road wheels with chamois-color spokes, and a decklid luggage rack with hold-down straps and bright buckles. Wheel choices for all models now included "lacy spoke" aluminum rims in chrome or white. A Corvette-style T-top roof with twin lift-off glass panels was a new option for fastbacks.

Still available for '77 was the useful Rallye Equipment Package for V-6 and V-8 models. This grouped the competition suspension with Traction-Lok limited-slip differential, white-letter tires, an "extra-cooling" package, chrome-tipped dual exhausts, color-keyed door mirrors, and a leather-

This page: Model-year 1976 brought no changes to the basic Mustang II lineup. The bread-and-butter notchback coupe (shown) poked along with the overhead-cam four-cylinder engine. With fuel mileage still on the minds of some shoppers, Ford tacked on the MPG suffix on all four-cylinder Mustang IIs. *Opposite page:* Purists blanched when Ford added the Shelby-like Cobra II package for 1976 fastbacks, but the option proved quite popular—even though it did nothing for acceleration. For $325, buyers got blue racing stripes on a white body, front and rear spoilers, a nonfunctional hood scoop, rear quarter-window louvers, dual sport mirrors, styled steel wheels with trim rings, white-letter tires, special interior trim, and Cobra II emblems. *Bottom right:* Another new tape-and-stripe job for 1976 was the Stallion. The package included a black grille, black moldings and windshield wiper arms, black paint on the lower body and bumpers, styled steel wheels, and big horse-head front-fender graphics. It was available on both Mustang II body styles and in four colors, but silver fastbacks like this one were the most common.

Opposite page: Trim options aside, Mustang II styling was unchanged after 1974. This Mach 1 wears non-stock driving lights ahead of a Cobra II-style front air dam. Factory options here include the desirable 302 V-8 and the Rallye Performance Package with raised-white-letter tires on styled steel wheels, plus three-spoke sports steering wheel and brushed-aluminum dashboard accents. By this time, all fastbacks came with a fold-down rear seat, which enhanced the cargo room and carrying versatility of the hatchback body style. This page, left: Cobra IIs added color choices for '77, including this arresting black-and-gold combo that recalled the '66 Shelby GT-350H Hertz Rent-a-Car. Bottom: Mustang II coupes could gain back some of the cargo versatility they lost to the fastback models via an optional luggage rack, which also lent a "neo-classic" vibe.

rim steering wheel. Mustang II may have been "less ponycar," but not when it came to options. Among those not already mentioned: anti-theft alarm, electric rear-window defroster, flip-out rear-quarter windows for fastbacks, fold-down rear seat for notchbacks (standard on fastbacks), center console, and the usual power assists. The worthwhile competition suspension added only $25–$60 depending on model and year.

Joining the Cobra II package for swan-song '78 was an even more garish King Cobra option. Again limited to fastbacks, it furnished a giant snake decal on the hood, tape stripes most everywhere else, black-finish exterior trim, and large "King Cobra" legends on doors, a deep front air dam, and a standard rear spoiler. Also included were the 302 V-8, power steering, Rallye Package, and 70-series radial tires. Subtle it wasn't, but at least the V-8 could deliver 17-second quarter-mile times, which was "high performance" for the day. At the other extreme was a new female-oriented Fashion Accessory Package that accessorized base notchbacks with door

pockets, striped fabric upholstery, lighted vanity mirror, and a four-way manual driver's seat.

Otherwise, the '78s were much like earlier Mustang IIs. Even so, model-year production rebounded to 192,410 units. The total would have been higher, but low dealer inventory prompted Ford to send out some '78s for sale as '77s.

Despite its commercial success, the Mustang II symbolizes a low period in Detroit history and has always been overshadowed by the more-exciting Ford ponycars that came before and after it. No wonder you seldom see one in good condition now, let alone at gatherings of the Mustang faithful. Too bad. As the late funny man Rodney Dangerfield would say, it deserves a little respect.

Both pages: The somewhat surprising popularity of the Cobra II package prompted Ford to offer an even more outlandish option for 1978. Though arguably over the top, the King Cobra wasn't entirely for show, as a 139-hp 302 V-8, power steering, power front disc brakes, and handling-oriented suspension were included in the asking price. However, that price was $1253—about a third of the cost of a base '78 Mustang II fastback. The gaudy spoilers, stripes, optional window louvers, and giant snake decal on the hood seemed rather "Seventies psychedelic," but interior decor was tasteful and included aluminum accents, console, and sports steering wheel. Today, the King Cobra's kitsch value places it among the most celebrated models of the largely unheralded Mustang II era.

6

Mustang began a second revolution with the
handsome, sophisticated "New Breed" of 1979. It
was clearly a new kind of Ford ponycar, yet in its
sporty elegance and appealing versatility, it was
every inch a Mustang, as appealing for its time as
the original was for the Sixties.

1979-1981: BACK ON TRACK

Work on the Mustang II's replacement began in April 1975, not long after Americans endured an unprecedented "energy crisis" with widespread fuel shortages and rising gasoline prices. (Another crunch followed in late 1979.) Not surprisingly, development emphasized improved fuel economy by reducing gas-wasting weight and aerodynamic drag (wind resistance). Dull though that may sound, the result was anything but. The 1979 Mustang (no more Roman numeral) was as right for its time as the original had been for the mid-1960s. Ford's ponycar was back on track. Even the running-horse logo looked like its old self.

From the first, this new Mustang was slated to share the unibody platform of the "Fox" compact cars that were developed in tandem with the ponycar and emerged as the 1978 Ford Fairmont/Mercury Zephyr. As with previous Mustangs, basic styling was selected from proposals submitted by competing in-house teams. The winner—and surprisingly

little altered for production—came from a group led by Jack Telnack, then executive director of Ford's North American Light Truck and Car Design. Like the original Mustang but unlike the II, the notchback coupe was done first and a sloped-roof hatchback evolved from it.

The quest for better fuel economy was partly driven by the federal Corporate Average Fuel Economy legislation prompted by the energy crisis. Taking effect with 1978 models, CAFE mandated that all vehicles sold by a given manufacturer must average so many EPA-rated miles per gallon each year, with the targets rising over time. Companies whose "fleet average" fell below a target would be fined for each 0.1-mpg deviation—multiplied by total sales for that model year. Makers exceeding a target earned "credits" that could be carried forward or backward to offset non-compliance in another year. Though controversial, CAFE did encourage development of more fuel-efficient vehicles.

Riding a 100.4-inch wheelbase (versus 105.5 for Fairmont/Zephyr), the '79 Mustang had a slightly wedge-shaped profile with a hood sloped down from a high cowl. Though this dictated unique inner front-fender aprons and radiator supports, Ford approved the extra cost for the sake of aerodynamics and thus fuel economy. Extensive wind-tunnel testing led to small spoilers front and rear. Drag coefficients were 0.44 for the hatchback and 0.46 for the notchback, good numbers for the time.

Body engineering aimed at minimizing weight to maximize both mileage and performance, so plastics, aluminum, and high-strength/low-alloy steel were used extensively. As a result, the '79 was some 200 pounds lighter than a comparable Mustang II despite being slightly larger outside. It also claimed 14–16 cubic feet more total interior volume and 2–4 cubic feet more cargo space. There were four trim levels: base, Sport Option, luxury Ghia, and sporty Cobra. The last stood apart with black-finish greenhouse trim and rocker panels, color-keyed body moldings, an optional snake decal for the hood, and jazzy cabin decor.

Marketing considerations also dictated three suspension "levels." The basic hardware was Fairmont/Zephyr, which meant modified MacPherson-strut geometry in front instead of conventional A-arms. Unlike other such setups, the coil spring did not encircle the strut but mounted between a lower arm and the body, which made replacing shock absorbers less expensive. An anti-roll bar was included. Rear geometry was a "four-bar link" arrangement, also with coil springs, lighter and more compact than Mustang II's leaf-spring setup. A rear anti-roll bar was included on some models. Suspension tuning took account of specific tires: bias-plys for the standard package, regular radials for the "handling" option. An enthusiast-oriented "special suspension" employed Michelin's sticky new TRX radials with a 390-mm diameter that required metric-size forged-aluminum wheels. This gave the tightest handling via the stiffest damping, a 1.12-inch front stabilizer bar, and a rear bar. Variable ratio rack-and-pinion steering was retained for all models.

This page: These early concept sketches by light-car design chief Fritz Mayhew helped point the way toward 1979 Mustang styling. Note the low, slim noses tapered down sharply from the windshield, plus the glassy rooflines and traditional long-hood/short-deck proportions. *Opposite page, top left:* A clay model from very early in the program shows a roofline perhaps inspired by that of Chevy's soon-to-appear 1975 Monza 2+2. *Top right:* The '79 Mustang was initially seen as just a sporty version of the emerging Fox-based Fairmont sedan. These proposals have a "little jewel" Mustang II flavor. *Bottom left:* A September 1975 trial shows rounded contours, thick lower-body cladding, and an awkward roofline that eventually gave way to a crisp, clean, "wedgy" notchback. *Bottom right:* Here, a '79 Mustang mock-up and a Mustang II lead a parade of proposals for what was likely an unrelated small-car program.

Engine choices reprised a standard 2.3-liter "Lima" four with 88 horsepower and included an intriguing new turbocharged version with 131 hp. Turbo engines were pretty exotic in 1979, especially for a mass-market American car. To prevent possible damage, maximum boost was limited to six psi by a "wastegate" relief valve that diverted the driving exhaust gases past the turbo. The venerable 302 V-8 returned with a 140 hp and a new low-restriction exhaust system. Mustang II's German-sourced V-6 was in short supply, so the old 200 inline-six, now rated at only 85 hp, was brought back to replace it late in the run. The V-8 and both sixes were available with a new four-speed gearbox, basically a three-speed manual with a long-striding overdrive tacked on. Self-shift Cruise-O-Matic remained optional as well.

Road tests praised the '79s as more agile and fun than Mustang IIs—especially a V-8 or turbo with the TRX chassis—but found acceleration wasn't improved so much. The typical V-8 model ran 0–60 mph in about nine seconds. The four-speed/V-6 was still in the 13–14 second range, while a like-equipped turbo four did the trip in 12–12.5 seconds.

Opposite page: As with past Mustangs, '79 styling was chosen from proposals submitted by competing teams—three in Dearborn, plus the Ford-owned Ghia studio in Italy. Each group had its own ideas, but all worked from the same set of "hard points," most of which reflected the planned sharing of chassis and some inner structure with the new compact Fairmont sedans and wagon. Once approved, the '79 styling was refined in the wind tunnel to trim air drag and thus enhance fuel economy. *This page, top:* Unlike Mustang II, the '79 was designed as a notchback. It's shown here in base four-cylinder form. *Right:* Ford pushed a performance theme for the '79 Mustang, but with an emphasis on handling rather than horsepower. The top engine choice was a two-barrel 302-cid V-8 with 140 horsepower.

The new Mustangs met the press in June 1978. A month later, Lee Iacocca was fired as Ford Motor Company president. The official reason was early retirement (on October 15, his 54th birthday), but many insiders suspected he'd be dumped before Henry Ford II retired as CEO in 1980 and as chairman in '82. As usual, HFII didn't say much. Neither did Iacocca—at first. Later he declared, "You just surmise that [HFII] doesn't want strong guys around." But Chrysler Corporation needed them badly, so after 32 years with Ford, Iacocca signed on as Chrysler president and then chairman, promising to pull that company out of its latest financial quagmire.

Helped by a generally strong market, '79 Mustang production totaled 332,025, a substantial gain on '78. Then came "Energy Crisis II" and a

sharp recession that crippled the U.S. economy—and sales at most every automaker. Mustang was no exception, as 1980-model production plunged 27 percent to 241,064 units.

The cars themselves weren't greatly changed—no surprise for a new design in its second year—but there were a few surprises. One involved the 302 V-8, which was replaced by a debored 255-cid version with 117 hp. Though it seemed an amazingly fast response to the second gas crunch, it had been planned long before in light of CAFE. And, of course, it did nothing for performance.

On the brighter side, Ford had finagled Mustang's selection as 1979 Indy 500 pace car, so a replica was a natural midyear addition. Ford sold some 11,000 of them with turbo-four or 302 V-8 power, then applied their

special styling touches—except race-related decals—to the 1980 Cobra. Those features comprised a slat grille, larger front and rear spoilers, integral foglamps, and a nonfunctioning hood scoop. Still built around the turbo-four and TRX suspension, the Cobra option was unavailable for notchbacks. A large snake decal for the hood remained a separate extra.

In other 1980 news, high-back vinyl bucket seats and color-keyed interior trim became standard linewide, as did brighter halogen headlights (supplanting conventional tungsten sealed-beams). Hatchbacks now came standard with Sport Option content, gaining styled wheels with trim rings, black rocker and window moldings, wide bodyside moldings, and sports steering wheel. Ghias again featured low-back vinyl buckets with headrests, door map pockets, thicker carpeting, and passenger-assist grips. A surprising new option was genuine Recaro front seats, as used on the '79 Pace Car Replica. With their infinitely variable backrest recliners and adjustable thigh and lumbar supports, Mustang now rivaled costly European cars for seat comfort.

Opposite page: Mustang was chosen as pace car for the 1979 Indy 500, and Ford celebrated by running off some 11,000 replicas. All were silver with orange, red, and black graphics, front and rear spoilers, sunroof, and the buyer's choice of a turbo four or 302 V-8. Pictured here are Mustang designer Jack Telnack (right) and other Ford executives with a prototype pace car. *This page, right and bottom left:* "New Breed" Mustang styling was little changed for sophomore 1980, but this "carriage roof" was newly available to give notchbacks the top-up look of a true convertible—right down to a simulated rear-window zip. *Bottom right:* The base "notchback" coupe was again the most popular Mustang for 1980, though output dropped to 128,893.

Opposite page, top left: The racy Cobra package was updated for 1980 via a slat grille, deep front airdam, and reverse-facing hood scoop, all picked up from the '79 Pace Car Replica. Top right: The "New Breed" interior showed as much European influence as the exterior, with standard full instrumentation and handy steering-column stalk controls for wipers and lights. Optional cruise control was operated from slim buttons on the steering wheel as shown here. Bottom: Optional vinyl roof, wire wheel covers, and white-wall tires spiff up this 1980 notchback. This page: A decade after abandoning motorsports, Ford hinted at an imminent return with the 1980 Mustang IMSA concept. Named for the International Motor Sports Association, whose GT racing series was a natural Mustang playground, this one-of-a-kind hatchback looked competition-ready with fat Pirelli tires on wildly dished wheels, plus muscular fender bulges, deep front airdam, loop rear spoiler, and eye-bending stripes. The similarly tricked-out interior featured Recaro seats with four-point harnesses, steering-wheel-mounted control buttons, and fluorescent instrument-panel lighting under a smoked-plastic cover.

Save the smaller V-8, Mustang's 1980 drivetrain chart was a photocopy of the late '79 lineup. Both fours again had a conventional four-speed manual gearbox as standard. The six came with the manual-overdrive transmission. Cruise-O-Matic remained mandatory with the V-8 and optional elsewhere.

Though "Total Performance" was a distant memory in 1980, Ford hinted that it would soon go racing again, with Mustang leading the way. One such teaser was the Mustang IMSA, a racy concept car powered by a much-modified turbo four. The name referenced the International Motor Sports Association GT series. Then, in September, Ford announced formation of Special Vehicle Operations under Michael Kranefuss, who'd been serving as competition director for Ford Europe. SVO's mission was to devise "a series of limited-production performance cars and develop their image through motorsport."

Opposite page, left: Ford PR photographed this Mustang trio for 1981 press-kit purposes. A sunroof-equipped hatchback sits above Sport Option and T-top notchbacks. Styling was again little changed for '81, but so was the broad options list that gave Mustang such wide appeal. *Top right:* The notchback's optional carriage roof continued for '81. *Bottom right:* Announced in late 1980, the M81 McLaren Mustang teamed Ford Design with McLaren Performance of Formula 1 racing fame. Just a handful of these $25,000 machines were built, all with turbo-four engines featuring a competition-style variable boost control, plus chassis and body mods clearly designed for the racetrack. *This page:* Though not predictive, the 1981 RSX concept showed how Ford's Ghia studio in Italy might handle a Mustang. Built on a shortened stock chassis with turbo-four power, the Rally Sport Experimental boasted angular "aero" lines, vivid orange-pearl metallic paint, and simulated all-glass doors.

As if to signal its racing intentions, Ford introduced the M81 McLaren Mustang in late 1980. Developed by Todd Gerstenberger and Harry Wykes, it looked somewhat like the IMSA concept but was more easily adapted to track work. It also carried a turbo-four, but with a new variable-boost control providing maximum pressure of 5–11 psi versus a fixed 5 psi. Horsepower at 10 psi was rated at 175, a considerable jump over the stock mill's typical 131-hp estimate (Ford never released an official rating for that engine). A $25,000 price tag and virtual hand construction limited production to only 10, including the prototype.

All this muscle-flexing had no affect on the 1981 Mustangs, which saw few changes. Reclining backrests were added to the standard bucket seats, interior trim was upgraded, and a T-bar roof with twin lift-off glass panels returned to the options list. The turbo-four was now limited to manual transmission only.

An optional five-speed overdrive manual had been announced for both Mustang fours in mid-1980 and became more widely available for '81. This pulled a shorter final drive for better off-the-line snap than the four-speed, and its overdrive fifth was geared for economical highway cruising. It was just what the base Mustang needed—except that, as Consumer Guide® noted, shift action was "stiff, yet vague" and fifth was "awkwardly located at the bottom of the dogleg to the right of and opposite fourth....Why Ford did it this way is a mystery....Our guess is that the engineers wanted to prevent inexperienced drivers from accidentally engaging overdrive and needlessly lugging the engine, as well as to prevent confusion with the often-used third. If so, they've succeeded admirably." Ford argued the U-shaped shift motion would better emphasize the economy benefits of the overdrive fifth. Whatever the reason, it just didn't work.

But such annoyances would soon be forgotten. Detroit performance was about to make an unexpected comeback, and Mustang would lead the charge.

7

When the going gets tough, the tough go racing—or
so said the new hard chargers who took command
at Ford during the rough times of the early 1980s.
But they knew "Total Performance" had worked
sales magic before. Why not again?

1982-1986: GALLOPING ON

The second energy crisis lasted little longer than the first, and gas was flowing again by 1982. Though the economy would remain mired in recession for a while, Detroit started emphasizing performance again, a coincidental result of decisions made before the 1980–81 oil shortage. Meantime, Ford Motor Company had weathered a major financial crisis and in 1980 secured two outstanding leaders to take over for Henry Ford II: Philip Caldwell as chairman and Donald Petersen as president. Petersen was a knowledgeable "car guy," and his enthusiasm influenced a reborn 1982 Mustang GT with a more-potent small-block V-8. This High-Output 302 delivered 157 net horsepower via a special camshaft, larger two-barrel carb, bigger and smoother exhaust, and low-restriction twin-inlet air cleaner. Teamed exclusively with four-speed overdrive manual transmission, it made for the quickest Mustang in years. Looking much like the Cobra package it replaced, the '82 GT came as a hatchback offering

premium TRX suspension, front and rear spoilers, foglamps, console, and other goodies for a reasonable $8308. The HO was optional for other models, but GTs probably accounted for the bulk of sales.

There was little other news for '82. Trim levels were renamed L, GL, and GLX in ascending order of price and luxury, and all models got wider rolling stock. The trouble-prone turbo-four engine was withdrawn, but other drivetrains returned. The 4.2-liter V-8's "mandatory option" automatic got a fuel-saving lockup torque converter effective in all forward gears, a device fast spreading throughout Detroit.

Smaller, third-generation General Motors ponycars arrived for '82, but Mustang managed fairly well for a three-year old design. Model-year production totaled about 130,418 against some 179,000 Chevrolet Camaros and 116,000 Pontiac Firebirds. The GT managed well in "buff" magazine showdowns with the rival 5.0-liter Camaro Z28 and Firebird

This page, left: Ford planned no big, immediate styling alterations for the Fox Mustang, but easy-change items would be redone from time to time. Shown here is an August 1980 shot of two future wheel cover ideas. The three-blade design at right would be base-model rim wear for 1983. *Below:* A late-August 1980 comparison of the rare and racy McLaren Mustang (left) and two workouts for the production '82 GT with rejected hood scoop and lower valence ideas. *Bottom:* Tail styling for the '82 GT was already decided by this time. Note the monogrammed taillight panel and the trunk-mounted fuel filler on the McLaren Mustang in the background. *Opposite page:* Mustang again listed several roof options for 1982. This advertising shot highlights the T-bar roof with twin liftoff glass panels. Its price that year was $1021.

Trans Am. The GM cars won points for style and handling, but the Mustang was usually judged better overall. And it was discernibly quicker. *Car and Driver* reported a 0–60 time of 8.1 seconds versus 8.6 for a fuel-injected automatic Camaro with automatic and 10.6 for a carbureted manual Firebird.

Seeking to close the handling gap with GM, the 1983 GT offered 220/55R390 Michelin TRX tires as a new option, plus a larger rear anti-roll bar among several suspension tweaks and higher-effort power steering for better high-speed control. The HO V-8 was boosted to 175 hp via a four-barrel carb, aluminum intake manifold, high-flow air cleaner, and larger exhaust passages. And it now mated to Borg-Warner's T-5 close-ratio five-speed gearbox, as in the Camaro/Firebird.

Elsewhere for '83, the 4.2 V-8 was dropped and the 200-cubic-inch straight six gave way to Ford's new lightweight "Essex" V-6, a 3.8-liter (232-cid) pushrod design with 105 hp. The base 2.3-liter four went from two-barrel to single-barrel carburetion for better mpg and adopted long-reach spark plugs for reduced emissions and improved drivability. Though these changes boosted alleged horsepower to 93, the rating would fall back to 88 hp for '84.

A mild facelift gave all '83s a more-aerodynamic nose with blue Ford ovals instead of running-horse emblems. Sun-worshippers cheered the first Mustang convertible in 10 years. Arriving as a GLX available with most powertrains, it was a factory job, not an outsourced conversion like some other reborn ragtops of the period.

The lineup expanded further at mid-1983 with a Turbo GT hatchback featuring a reengineered version of the hyperaspirated 2.3 "Lima" four. Major changes from '81 involved switching to Bosch port electronic fuel injection and repositioning the turbocharger to "blow through" the intake system instead of "draw down" from it. Ford's latest EEC-IV electronic engine-control system governed injector timing, idle speed, wastegate, and emissions-related components. Other upgrades included forged-aluminum pistons, lighter flywheel, and engine oil cooler. For all that, the new turbocharged four claimed only five more horsepower than the previous engine, 145 in all.

Aside from nameplates, the Turbo GT was a visual twin to the V-8 model. Both came with specific suspension tuning, beefy Goodyear Eagle performance radials, aluminum wheels, sport bucket seats, and five-speed manual. With the same advertised power as a base Z28, the Turbo GT could run 0–60 mph in well under 10 seconds and the standing quarter mile in about 16 while returning 25 mpg overall. But it remained a tough sell. The '83 wasn't available with air conditioning or automatic—a big drawback for most buyers—and it cost $250 more than a comparable V-8 GT, which could hit 60 in near six seconds flat. Model-year sales were predictably paltry: just 483. Total Mustang deliveries slid seven percent to 120,873, reflecting an overall market still stymied by recession.

Despite the Turbo GT's dismal sales, its engine was further massaged for yet another new performance Mustang, the 1984 SVO. Named for and engineered by Ford's Special Vehicle Operations department, this exotic new hatchback sported an air-to-air intercooler and electronically variable boost control allowing up to 14 psi. These and other changes produced a remarkable 175 hp, plus 10 percent more torque, delivered through a

Opposite page, top and bottom: Announcing Ford's sudden but welcome return to hot street cars, the 1982 GT hatchback was the quickest Mustang in years. At $8308, it was also top of the line, but its new 157-horsepower 302 V-8 was optional for other models at $402–$452. Functional hood scoop (shown at top, with McLaren Mustang) cost $38. *This page, top right and left:* To accompany the introduction of the Mustang GT, Ford put a Mustang convertible on the auto-show circuit and announced it would be available in late summer with the 5.0 HO engine. However, production was delayed until the 1983 model year. *Right:* For '83, Mustang convertibles were offered only in upscale GLX or GT trim. The GLX's interior (shown here) was plenty sporty, and came with a standard four-speed gearbox (five-speed optional) when the 5.0 was ordered. V-6s had automatic. First-year ragtop sales far surpassed Ford's estimates.

five-speed gearbox with Hurst linkage and a Traction-Lok limited-slip differential.

The SVO boasted larger front-disc brakes and beefy rear discs instead of drums, plus 16 X 7-inch "aero-style" cast-aluminum wheels with meaty V-rated European Goodyear NCT radials, later switched to Eagle GT50s with unidirectional "gatorback" tread. Spring rates and bushings were much stiffened, premium adjustable Koni shocks were specified, the front anti-roll bar was thickened, a rear bar was added, and power steering was changed from variable-ratio to fast fixed-ratio gearing.

Visually, the SVO stood apart with a "biplane" rear spoiler, unique "grille-less" nose, a large hood scoop feeding the intercooler, dual square headlamps instead of smaller quads, a deep front airdam incorporating standard foglamps, and small fairings to smooth airflow around the rear wheels. Driver-oriented cabin accoutrements included a left footrest,

multi-adjustable seats, and leather-rim tilt steering wheel. There were only five major options: air, power windows, cassette player, flip-up glass sunroof, and leather upholstery.

The SVO was the most "European" Mustang yet. Handling was near-neutral, cornering flat and undramatic, steering direct and properly weighted, braking swift and sure. Performance was exhilarating: 0–60 in about 7.5 seconds, the quarter-mile in just under 16 at around 90 mph. Alas, this was just another sophisticated screamer that only hardcore "gearheads" would buy. At more than $16,000, the SVO looked too costly when a V-8 GT delivered for a whopping $6000 less. Sales thus totaled only 4508 for model-year '84, though Ford had the capability to build nearly four times that many.

Between them, the SVO and V-8 GT killed off the Turbo GT after some 3000 hatchbacks and about 600 convertibles were built for 1983–84. All

Opposite page, left: The '83s boasted a smart new "aero" face and many detail improvements, but model-year sales hit a decade low of just under 121,000. Demand soon picked up in a reviving economy where gas was again plentiful and cheap. GLX hatchbacks like this one started at $7439. Right: The lack of fender badges means that this Mustang ragtop carries the standard V-6; a four-cylinder was not available in this body style. This page, top left and right: Aluminum wheels are the tip-off that these two 5.0 Mustang convertibles are equipped with the TRX suspension package. Right: GTs got a more-aggressive look for 1983 via a "power bulge" hood with a broad black stripe. The HO added 18 horsepower this year via internal tweaks and a deeper-breathing four-barrel carb instead of a 2V. A new close-ratio five-speed transmission further improved performance.

This page, left: Ford revived a turbo Mustang in mid-'83, using the turbocharged 145-hp 2.3-liter four-cylinder shared with the handsome new Thunderbird Turbo Coupe. However, the Mustang Turbo GT was a poor seller, being slower and costlier than the V-8 GTs. *Bottom left and right:* Mustang marked 20 years with a modest trim option for the 1984 V-8 GT convertible (here with a classic 64½) and hatchback. Mustang traditionalists were happy to see the tri-color running-horse badge return. Finished in Oxford White with Canyon Red stripes and interior, this GT-350 package prompted a lawsuit from Carroll Shelby, who said Ford broke a promise in using the name without his permission. Ford settled. *Opposite page:* Just 3900 of the 20th anniversary hatchbacks were produced. This one has the 5.0-liter V-8, but the turbo four was also available.

early-'84 GTs were '83 reruns save a split rear seatback (as adopted for most hatchbacks that year). The Turbo GT ragtop arrived in December '83, when all GTs received staggered rear shocks, integral foglamps, and a restyled rear spoiler. Also new for '84: a base-trim hatchback to complement the entry-level notchback; GL and GLX equipment combined into one LX trim level; and new GT and LX convertibles. There was also a second 302 V-8, with throttle-body fuel injection (TBI) and 10 fewer horses than the HO. It was reserved for non-GTs with optional automatic, which was now either a three-speed or Ford's new corporate four-speed overdrive unit—another CAFE-inspired development. The V-6 option also got TBI and went to 120 hp; it paired only with the three-speed automatic.

Mustang was 20 years old in 1984, and Ford celebrated with 5000 GT-350 models—actually a GT trim option featuring "Shelby White" paint and maroon stripes. It was a nice remembrance, but Mr. Shelby claimed he owned "GT-350" and sued Ford for copyright infringement. On a happier note, Mustang sales rebounded to 141,480 units for '84 and would reach 156,514 for '85. By contrast, combined Camaro/Firebird volume began trending down and would be below Mustang's by 1987.

A key reason for that was that Mustang had become an uncommonly good sporty-car value. The '85 base-price range ran from just $6885 for the LX notchback to $13,585 for the GT ragtop and $14,521 for the slow-selling SVO. Though much higher than '79 stickers in raw dollars, those figures looked mighty attractive against Japanese sporty cars that were starting to gallop in price but couldn't match Mustang for performance or charisma.

Those qualities were further enhanced for '85. Low-friction roller tappets and a high-performance camshaft muscled up the carbureted HO V-8 by an impressive 35 hp, to 210. Similar changes took the injected version to 180. Both 302s again teamed only with five-speed manual, which got revised gearing and a redesigned linkage. Rounding out GT improvements were beefier P225/60VR15 "Gatorbacks" on seven-inch-wide aluminum wheels, as on the SVO, plus gas-pressure front shocks and an extra pair of rear shocks to control axle tramp.

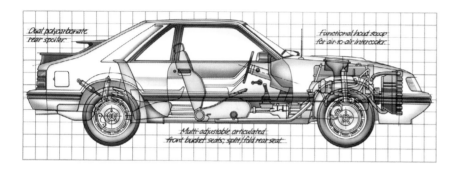

Opposite page: Mustang blazed a new performance trail with the 1984 SVO. A grille-less nose and "biplane" rear spoiler mimicked the look of Ford's sporty European Sierra XR4. A hood scoop fed air to a high-tech turbo four making 175 hp. *This page:* Mustang got another nose job for 1985, this time with a simple one-slot grille above an integrated bumper/spoiler. GT Mustangs like these could get fuel-injected or carbureted V-8s this year, with 180 or 210 hp, respectively.

This page, left: Despite few changes for 1986, Mustang notched decade-high model-year sales of nearly a quarter-million units. As before, "5.0" front-fender badges signaled V-8 power, as on this LX notchback. Below left: Mustang went to a single V-8 for 1986, a new 200-horsepower HO with electronic port fuel injection. Below right: At $14,523 to start, the GT convertible was the priciest '86 Mustang—except for the $15,272 swan-song SVO. Opposite page: Answering a request from the California Highway Patrol, Ford devised a high-speed Mustang pursuit package in 1983. Within three years, thousands of such cars were catching speeders in 14 other states. This one served in Florida.

All mainstream '85s adopted SVO-type nose styling except the cheap L models, which were dropped. The SVO itself returned at midyear with flush headlights (newly allowed by the government), plus an air-to-air intercooler that puffed up its turbo four by 30 hp, to 205. The intercooler also appeared on a revived Turbo GT that quickly vanished again after minuscule sales.

Mustang sales surged to 224,410 for 1986, a decade high achieved with few changes. The main one was adoption of sequential port injection for a single 302 V-8 rated at 200 hp and available with either five-speed manual or four-speed automatic. The rear axle was strengthened to handle V-8 torque that now peaked at a strong 285 pound-feet. The SVO's hydraulic engine mounts were added to all V-8 and V-6 models.

The inevitable yearly price increases were evident, but fairly modest. The notchback LX was up to $7295, the ragtop GT to $14,220. The SVO was costlier than ever at $15,272, but its days were numbered. With sales always far below even Ford's modest projections, it wasn't profitable enough to sustain, so '86 was its swan song. Respective 1985–86 production was 1954 and 3382.

If nothing else, the SVO demonstrated the performance potential of the basic Fox-platform design. And new excitement awaited as the original ponycar galloped toward its milestone 25th birthday.

Ford briefly considered revamping the Mustang as a Japanese-bred front-wheel-drive machine, but wisely nixed those plans. Instead, the old-soldier Fox-platform Mustang was kept as fresh as possible via careful styling and engineering updates.

1987–1993: FALSE START, FINE FINISH

Improbable as it may seem now, Mustang's future was suddenly unclear in the early 1980s, thanks in part to the sharp recession triggered by "Energy Crisis II." Though the Fox-platform design was still selling respectably, Dearborn knew it would need updating fairly soon. But with the economy showing faint signs of recovery, some in Dearborn began to worry about the inevitable next downturn and whether the traditional ponycar formula was still relevant.

Such was the atmosphere in early 1982 when planners began work on a next-generation Mustang as project SN8 (SN for "sporty, North America"). This envisioned a smaller, lighter ponycar like the Mustang II or European Capri, but with aero styling, front-wheel drive for maximum space inside, and high-efficiency four-cylinder engines instead of a thirsty V-8. Initial proposals failed to satisfy management, however, so just a year into the program Ford turned to Japanese partner Mazda, whose small-car expertise was at least equal to Ford's own.

Mazda was then planning a redesign of its compact front-drive 626 coupe, one of Mustang's new-wave rivals. Ford proposed sharing development expenses to produce a new 626-based Mustang. The economics appealed to Mazda, which had decided to set up a plant in Flat Rock, Michigan, near Ford's historic River Rouge factory. Mazda also saw the deal as a chance to score valuable public-opinion points. With "Japan Inc." taking big chunks out of Detroit's sales hide, Congress was threatening more protectionist legislation that the Japanese hoped to forestall with "transplant" operations like Flat Rock.

But Ford hadn't counted on the outrage of diehard Mustangers when word of the plan leaked out. A Japanese design? No way! And besides, front drive is for econoboxes, not "real cars." Ford listened and released the erstwhile "626 Mustang" (cousin to Mazda's MX-6) as the 1989 Probe.

The decision was wise. Though capable and spirited in turbocharged GT form, the Probe was too "foreign" to be accepted as an American product, even if it did have Ford styling.

In the aftermath, and with the recession starting to ease, Dearborn decided to keep the old Fox going until a "proper" replacement was ready. The result arrived for 1987 as the most fully overhauled Mustang since 1979. The slow-selling SVO was history (as was Mercury's related Capri, which hadn't sold as expected since its '79 reinvention), but LX and GT notchbacks, hatchbacks, and convertibles all returned. The basic shape was recognizable but slicker than ever, with a smoother nose, flush

headlamps, and, convertibles excepted, rear side glass pulled out flush with the body. The result was a more contemporary look that dropped drag coefficients to as low as 0.36.

As before, LXs were more visually restrained than GTs, using a simple "slot" grille containing a horizontal bar with a small blue oval. Below was a body-color bumper with integral spoiler and wide, wraparound black rubstrips that continued to a color-keyed rear bumper. GTs got flashy rocker-panel skirts, dummy scoops ahead of the rear wheels, busy "cheese grater" taillamps, and a grille-less nose with a wide "mouth" in a forward-jutting airdam, flanked by round foglamps. All models received a modern

Opposite page: Flush-mount headlamps, a legacy of the late Mustang SVO, gave all '87s a smoother, more coherent face. LXs like this four-cylinder ragtop had a simple central air slot instead of the GT's solid front fascia, but all models "breathed" mainly through an under-bumper intake. Multiport fuel injection was a new '87 upgrade for the 2.3-liter four, but horsepower and torque were only a little higher. *This page, right and below:* A growing number of Mustangers in '87 took their V-8 in one of the less-showy LX models like the notchback and hatchback shown here. *Below right:* Mustang's new '87 instrument panel was quite "international" in appearance and function with its useful package shelf, simple rotary climate controls, and BMW-style air vents.

new instrument panel with more-convenient controls, an expensive change that suggested the Fox-platform design would hang on a while longer—which it would.

The main mechanical alterations for '87 involved the venerable small-block V-8—no surprise, as it was now way ahead of the 2.3-liter four in customer preference. A return to freer-breathing, pre-1986 cylinder heads and other induction changes added 25 horsepower for a total of 225, thus matching the top Chevrolet Camaro/Pontiac Firebird option, a 5.7-liter Corvette mill. Torque was up as well, to a stout 300 pound-feet. The 5.0-liter/302 V-8 remained standard for GTs, which also received larger front-disc brakes and a recalibrated suspension. The lowly four exchanged a one-barrel carburetor for multipoint electronic fuel injection, but was hardly more potent at 90 hp and 130 pound-feet. At least it now teamed with standard five-speed manual or optional four-speed automatic transmissions (replacing a four-speed stick and three-speed slushbox), which helped maximize what little power it had. A big surprise was the deletion of the optional 3.8 V-6, leaving a huge power and performance gap between the four and the V-8.

Opposite page, top and bottom left: For 1987, Ford Design styled the GT for an "increased differential" from the rest of the Mustang lineup. Opinions divided over the style merits of the GT's deep perimeter "skirts" and busy "cheese-grater" taillights, but most everyone liked the handsome new wheels. A smoother new nose helped lower the GT hatchback's drag coefficient to a worthy 0.38. *Top right:* Mustang's trusty 302 V-8 was muscled up again for 1987, tacking on 25 horsepower for a total of 225. A return to freer-breathing cylinder heads and other induction changes did the trick. *This page, above and bottom right:* An '87 GT convertible started at $15,724—almost $7700 more than a base four-cylinder notchback coupe. In place of the GT hatchback's spoiler, GT ragtops wore a rear-deck luggage rack. *Top right:* In addition to the handsome instrument panel, all-new Mustang interiors featured long armrests, a reworked console, and GT-standard "articulated" front seats with power-operated lumbar support.

This page, left: Ford spent some $200 million on Mustang's 1987 restyle, so no one was surprised when the '88s arrived looking exactly the same. Prices continued an upward gallop from '87, rising another $700–$1100. This four-cylinder notchback now started at $8726. *Below:* Mustang's T-top option did not return for '88, due in part to continuing strong convertible sales. *Opposite page:* A 1989 GT ragtop sidles next to a classic 1964½ in a widely circulated Ford PR photo announcing Mustang's 25th anniversary.

A lot of '87 V-8s were ordered with LX trim via an $1885 package that also included the GT's uprated chassis and rolling stock. In fact, demand for 5.0-liter LXs proved so strong that Ford briefly ran short of engines, telling customers who wanted a V-8 Mustang that they'd have to take a GT. Not surprisingly, this did not go over well. For some buyers, the facelifted GT was either ugly, outlandish, or both, which must have dismayed Jack Telnack, who was named overall Ford Design chief in mid-1987. Others simply preferred the quieter LX styling because it was less likely to attract unwanted attention from law-enforcement.

Regardless, the fortified small-block delivered performance recalling the good old days: 0–60 mph, for instance, now took slightly less than six seconds. Technology was allowing Ford (and others) to do what had once been achievable only with cubic inches and hot-rodder tricks. To get 225 net horsepower in, say, a '72 Mustang required the optional 351 V-8

This page: After five years of building V-8 Mustangs with racier looks and trackworthy chassis, Southern California's Steve Saleen offered his first "tuned" Mustang, the SSC. Introduced on April 17, 1989, Mustang's exact 25th birthday, it packed 292 horsepower—67 more than stock—yet was street-legal in all states, quite a feat for a small company like Saleen Autosport. Special bracing in the engine and cargo bays made for a solid driving feel and more precise handing. Saleen built only 161 SSCs in '89, all hatchbacks. *Opposite page, left:* Arriving in January 1990, this "Limited Edition" LX 5.0 convertible boasted unique Deep Emerald Green metallic paint complemented by a white leather interior and color-keyed top boot. Base price was a stiff $18,949. *Right:* Mustang's steadily improved workmanship was especially evident inside. Optional leather, as shown here, returned for 1990 at $489.

(168–275 net hp). Yet the '87 engine was thriftier and smoother, needed less upkeep, and was more reliable.

Progress often carries a price, of course, but Mustang remained an exception. As Consumer Guide® said at the time, "Though far from perfect—or perfected—the ['87] Mustang GT is put together well enough and offers a ton of go for your dough....Despite a full option load—air, premium sound system, cruise control, and power windows, door locks, and mirrors—our [hatchback] came to $14,352, which is an exceptional value when IROC-Z Camaros, Toyota Supras, and Nissan 300ZXs can go for $5000 more."

But a better car doesn't necessarily guarantee better sales, and Mustang deliveries crumbled by more than 65,000 units for 1987, even though the economy was again humming along. Still, 159,145 total sales was good going, all things considered. And despite the lower volume, Ford ponied up some $200 million that year to upgrade the River Rouge plant (by now the only facility building Mustangs), a move that doubtless cheered the car's millions of fans.

Mustang was virtually unchanged for 1988, yet sales rebounded to 211,225. The following year, Ford standardized power windows for convertibles and made the LX V-8 package a full-fledged series labeled LX 5.0L Sport (with standard GT seats as a bonus). Despite another same-again season, sales declined only a little, falling to 209,769.

But wait: 1989 was Mustang's 25th anniversary. Time for a birthday commemorative, right? Well, yes and no. Ford planned one, a hot GT assigned to favored independent tuner Jack Roush, but development delays and fuel-economy mandates killed it. Instead, Ford issued 3800 Emerald Green V-8 LX convertibles starting in mid-January 1990, a minor observance for a major milestone.

Those cars and other 1990 Mustangs met a new federal rule for "passive restraints" with a driver-side airbag mounted in the steering wheel. Also added were clearcoat paint and optional leather upholstery. Prices remained attractive: under $9500 for a four-cylinder LX two-door, less than $19,000 for the GT ragtop. Even so, another recession had begun, and model-year production plunged nearly 50 percent to 128,189.

The '91 tally dropped 23 percent from there, to 98,737, partly because changes were again so few. The anemic four was boosted to 105 hp via a new eight-plug cylinder head, but only rental-car companies cared. Convertible tops were redesigned to fold down into a smaller "stack," and automatic-transmission cars met another new federal edict with a shift interlock that prevented moving out of Park without first applying the brakes. Prices rose a bit, the base LX two-door now starting at just over $10,000.

Even smaller changes occurred for '92, when Mustang sales withered to an all-time model-year low of 79,280. LXs were tidied up with color-keyed bodyside moldings and bumper rubstrips, and options no longer included whitewall tires and wire wheel covers.

The economy was perking up again by model-year 1993, and Mustang sales followed suit, rebounding to 114,228. In a way, this shouldn't have happened. For one thing, GM had a swoopy new fourth-generation Camaro/Firebird whose top power option was a 5.7-liter LT1 V-8 tuned for 275 hp. Worse, having admitted to overrating outputs of Mustang's V-8, Ford now advertised lower numbers of 205 hp and 275 pound-feet. Meanwhile, industry spies were reporting that work was fast winding up on the new Mustang that enthusiasts had been anticipating for at least five years.... Perhaps that moved some folks to buy a "last-gen" '93.

Ford provided its own incentive with a hot hatchback worthy of 25th

Opposite page, top: Mustang sales fell again for 1991, aggravated by a 3-percent price hike that put basic four-cylinder LXs like this hatchback over $10,000 for the first time. *Bottom:* A reworked top with a lower folded "stack height" tidied up the convertible's appearance. *This page:* V-8 sales had been steadily growing and were now two times that of four-cylinder models, split evenly between GTs and LXs. A 5.0 LX notchback is shown here. *Top right:* Pretty new five-spoke, 16-inch alloy wheels were a new standard for 1991 V-8 models, completed with the traditional "pony tri-color" insignia. *Right:* As always, the GT convertible offered fun in the sun—and most everywhere else. Still top of the line, it priced from $19,864 for '91.

This page and opposite page, top: Ford attempted to spice up its aging Mustang lineup with special appearance packages, all with color-keyed windshield frames, exclusive color treatments, and a unique decklid spoiler. The Performance Red package debuted in mid-1992; Vibrant White and Canary Yellow versions followed in 1993. *Opposite page, bottom:* The 1993 GT saw no changes of note, though Ford's revised method of rating horsepower downrated its 5.0 V-8 from 225 to 205.

Anniversary badges. But it wore the Cobra name and snake insignia of Carroll Shelby's legendary Mustang GTs, mainly so Ford could keep its legal claim to both from expiring for want of use. *Road & Track* called this Cobra the "best of an aging breed," and by most any measure it was. Developed by Dearborn's new Special Vehicle Team (SVT, the successor to SVO), it claimed 245 hp and 285 pound-feet from a 302 V-8 carrying special big-port "GT40" heads, tuned-runner intake manifold, revised cam, and other muscle-building enhancements. A beefier five-speed manual gearbox was mandatory, and standard tires were massive (for the day) 245/45ZR17 Goodyear Eagle performance radials. Also on hand, or rather underfoot, were rear-disc brakes instead of drums—making Cobra the first Mustang since the SVO to have them—plus more "balanced" suspension tuning that seemed to go against conventional wisdom with *softer* springs, shocks, and bushings and a *smaller* front stabilizer bar. Interior furnishings were everyday GT, but exterior details differed: SVO taillamps, handsome seven-blade alloy wheels, and an LX-style slot grille with a wee running-horse emblem. A prominent rear spoiler was the one arguably jarring note to this speedy, sophisticated package.

How speedy? *R&T*'s Cobra clocked 5.9 seconds 0–60 mph, an impressive 14.5 seconds at 98 mph in the standing quarter-mile, and under 16 seconds from 0 to 100. If this wasn't Sixties performance reborn, it was more than adequate for the Nineties. As for sophisticated, *Car and Driver* termed the Cobra "a nicer-riding, more supple car [than the GT]. Although it can feel less buttoned down...the Cobra makes better use of its tires and rewards coordinated hands and feet with clearly higher limits and cornering speeds...."

Nevertheless, cynics viewed this latest Mustang Cobra as a ploy to keep Ford's old ponycar from being overshadowed by GM's new ones. Indeed, *Motor Trend* called it a "shake-and-bake bridge to '94." Still, here was more eloquent testimony to the versatility of the Fox-platform design—and Ford's skill at keeping it competitive. And with only 4993 built, the '93

This page: Loyal Mustangers got a heartening 1993 surprise in the new SVT Cobra hatchback. Conceived by Ford's two-year-old Special Vehicle Team, the Cobra packed a 235-hp 5.0 V-8 and could sprint from 0 to 60 in under six seconds. Starting right at $20,000, it boasted 17-inch wheels, sticky Goodyear tires, a recalibrated chassis, and unique styling touches. Exactly 4993 were built. *Opposite page:* Perhaps to dispel any doubts about Mustang's future, Ford took this racy show car to various 1992 auto shows. Also created by SVT, the Mustang Mach III concept provided an exaggerated preview of next-generation Mustang styling. Designed with no thought of a top, the two-seat body was paneled in high-tech carbon fiber above 19-inch chrome wheels. A front-mounted 4.6-liter supercharged V-8 sent 450 horsepower through a six-speed manual gearbox. Ford claimed 0–60 mph in under five seconds.

Cobra quickly became a sought-after collectible.

Even more coveted was the Cobra R, which saw just 107 copies. As with the classic track-ready Shelby GT-350, the "R" meant racing. Alterations involved much larger front brakes, competition-caliber cooling system and suspension tuning, even bigger wheels and tires, and added structural reinforcements. Omitting the back seat, air conditioning, and most power accessories reduced curb weight by 60 pounds—not much on the street but enough to tell on the track. Ford sold every R model for the full $25,692 sticker price, versus about $20,000 for a "regular" Cobra, itself a bona fide bargain.

After this flurry of excitement, Ford was finally ready to start the next chapter in the Mustang saga. And what a surprising story it would turn out

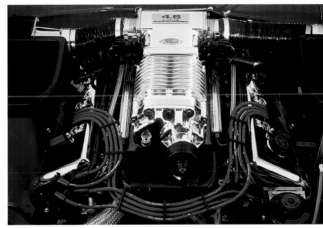

9

Hard to believe, but Ford actually thought of
putting Mustang out to pasture—until it learned of
General Motors' latest ponycar plans. Dearborn
met the challenge by keeping the best and
changing the rest to create a stronger, sleeker,
more agile new Mustang.

1994–1998: PAST FORWARD

A mostly new Mustang rode in for 1994 on a tidal wave of anticipation and nostalgia. Announcement ads pictured one with a classic '65 to declare "It is what it was." Actually, it almost wasn't at all.

The uproar over the Probe (see previous chapter) had shown that ponycar diehards wouldn't accept a Japanese-style substitute. Trouble was, demand for "real" ponycars was lagging again by the early '90s, leading some in Dearborn to ask once more if another new Mustang might ever be needed. Even if it were, Ford had more-profitable fish to fry—the hugely popular Explorer sport-utility vehicle for one. Besides, Mustang sales were still decent, so why rush?

With that, planning floundered for a good two years while the car's future was debated. (Shades of 1982.) Then Ford learned that General Motors was abandoning a planned front-wheel-drive Chevrolet Camaro/Pontiac Firebird for a new rear-drive 1993 concept. Corporate pride

demanded a proper reply, so Ford authorized work toward a new Mustang in 1991 as project SN95.

Because Ford had become a much leaner outfit, and with the "team concept" now gospel in Detroit, SN95 developed quite differently from earlier Mustangs. The big departure was forming a fairly small, independent multidiscipline group to herd the new pony from drawing board to showroom. Money matters dictated a surprisingly modest $700 million budget (versus $3 billion for the trendsetting midsize 1986 Taurus), of which only $200 million was earmarked for design and engineering. The deadline was equally tight: just 36 months.

Echoing past Mustang programs was the trio of mock-ups considered for SN95 styling. All had "retro" appearance cues, including a big galloping steed in the grille, plus a smooth, muscular, slightly wedgy shape as decreed by design chief Jack Telnack. Tamest of the three was the "Bruce

Jenner," a "trim, athletic" design that scored low in consumer polls for looking too "soft." At the other extreme was "Rambo," an aggressively exaggerated version that was rejected as too macho. This left the in-between "Arnold Schwarzenegger" to carry the day. All three finalists were modeled as "trunked" coupes. Though a new convertible was never in doubt, Americans no longer cared much for hatchbacks, so that body style was forgotten despite its importance to recent Mustang sales.

Interior designers also strove for a "classic" feel while building in new government-mandated safety features like dual dashboard airbags and anti-intrusion door beams. What emerged was the usual 2+2 package with a wildly sculpted "twin-cowl" instrument panel paying faint homage to the Sixties.

Because time and money precluded a full redesign, SN95 made do with a much-modified version of the veteran '79 platform dubbed "Fox-4." Body engineers worked hard to increase rigidity without appreciable weight gain, and succeeded. Against the previous notchback, the SN95 coupe was some 56 percent stiffer in bending resistance and 44 percent better in torsional strength; comparable convertible numbers were 76 percent and a startling 150 percent. Despite these impressive gains, curb weights rose by only some 280 pounds from equivalent '93s. Chassis engineers decreed softer damping, much-revised suspension geometry, and a 1.8-inch-longer wheelbase—to 101.5 inches. The new styling added 1.7 inches to overall length and 1.3 inches to width. Wheel/tire packages were upgraded. So were brakes, with larger front discs, newly standard rear discs, a bigger booster, and Bosch antilock control as a first-time option.

Powerteams were familiar fare. Base models, no longer called LX, traded the anemic four-cylinder for a standard 3.8-liter V-6, the same engine last offered for '86 but retuned for 145 hp. The LX 5.0L package was also dropped, leaving V-8 power the sole province of GT models. Though the venerable small-block was little changed from '93, it somehow gained 10 horses—for 240 total—and a like number of pound-feet, perhaps by the stroke of a pen. Transmissions again comprised five-speed manual or

S-32099-2

S-32099-16

Opposite page: Design work for the 1994 SN95 Mustang was underway by early 1989. Opinion data from consumer clinics showed strong preference for modern lines blended with traditional Mustang signatures, as shown in these early concept sketches. This page: SN95 styling came down to three full-size fiberglass mockups examined in fall 1990 by representatives of Ford marketing, sales, product development, and upper management. The "Bruce Jenner" (top left) was rejected as too tame. The aggressive "Rambo" (top right) and "Arnold Schwarzenegger" (right) ran about even in consumer clinics, but the Arnold was OKed for production with relatively few changes.

S-32099-24

This page, top left and left: Mustang's long-serving platform changed so much for 1994 that Ford renamed it "Fox-4." Ford built life-size cutaway displays to highlight the platform's extensive changes. Its floorpan (in white) was the major carryover structural component. Front X-brace (in yellow) was one of several measures enhancing overall rigidity. *Top right:* A cutaway illustration by artist David Kimble showcases '94 Mustang packaging on a V-6 coupe. *Opposite page:* Frequent "yesterday and today" photo ops showed that Ford continued to value (and capitalize on) Mustang's colorful heritage. In this family portrait, a GT convertible (foreground) poses with a base V-6 ragtop and a '65 ragtop. Only coupes and convertibles were offered now; the three-door hatchback was dropped because of the difficulty in building one with required levels of torsional stiffness. The LX model designation was also eliminated.

optional four-speed automatic, but the latter was Ford's latest "AOD-E" unit with electronic shift control.

Overall, the '94 Mustang seemed the same kind of unexpectedly thorough makeover that Dearborn had recently accorded its full-size sedans. Still, some were disappointed that the long-awaited new Mustang wasn't ground-up new, especially as some prices rose to the point of "sticker shock." The base coupe, for instance, jumped $2646 to $13,365, though that included a larger engine, better brakes and dual airbags,

This page, left: At $13,365, the '94 V-6 coupe started quite a bit higher than the former four-cylinder LX. *Bottom left:* Handsome new "twin-cowl" dashboards featured full instrumentation and dual airbags. *Bottom right:* V-6 and V-8 models each offered two different wheel treatments: 15-inchers for the V-6, and a 16-inch five-spoke or 17-inch six-spoke design for GTs. *Opposite page:* The running-horse grille badge made its return, and sculptured bodyside scoops and tri-segmented taillights also recalled Mustang's past. The 1994 GT's sole engine choice was an improved 5.0-liter V-8 with 215 horsepower.

plus a tilt steering wheel and power driver's seat, both options before. The GT coupe was up $1533 to $17,280, though it, too, claimed the same improvements. At least the base convertible looked a fine value at $20,160, and the GT edition was a reasonable $21,970. Both ragtops were again factory-built with standard power roof and glass rear window, which now included a rear defogger. An optional 80-pound lift-off hardtop was announced as a $1500 convertible option, but was never actually sold due to production glitches.

To Ford's undoubted dismay, the rejuvenated Mustang earned mixed reviews. While road-testers rightly lauded the many upgrades, there was general head-scratching over the GT's 60-hp deficit with the latest Camaro Z28 and Firebird Trans Am. "The carryover power may challenge the loyalty of some...fans," mused *Car and Driver*, "[though] with substantial improvements in braking and body structure, the Mustang [GT still] offers tremendous performance for the dollar." As if to prove the point, *C/D*'s

This page: Ford's SVT division put together another limited-edition Mustang Cobra for '94, set off by discreet Cobra fender badges, a Cobra-exclusive rear wing, unique 17 X 8-inch wheels, and white-faced gauges. Despite much massaging by SVT, the Cobra's 5.0 V-8 made only 5 horsepower more than the 1993 version. *Opposite page:* A '94 Cobra convertible paced the Indy 500 on May 29, 1994. It's posed here at the famous track with its '64½ and '79 predecessors.

five-speed coupe clocked 0–60 mph in just 6.1 seconds and the standing quarter-mile in 14.9 at 93 mph—not bad for a 30-year-old engine. The automatic version was no slouch either, Consumer Guide®'s coupe running 0–60 in a brisk 7.4 seconds.

Still, the power/performance gap with GM suggested sights had not been set very high. And indeed, Dearborn admitted that the '94 was designed mainly to please the 6.1 million people who'd bought Mustangs since day one. From a sales standpoint, that wasn't a bad plan. As *Motor Trend* observed: "Mustang fans have been deprived of a new platform for so long they would've accepted almost anything with a chrome horse on it." And of course, they did accept it—certainly more enthusiastically than some of the press. But why not? They had, after all, helped to design it. As a thank you, Ford hosted regional parties for Mustang clubs on Sunday, April 17, 1994, exactly 30 years since the original Mustang's smash debut.

THE **BOSS** IS BACK.

Opposite page, top left: Mustang entered 1995 as the most popular ponycar in America. With a new generation introduced for '94 and the factory unable to keep up with demand, changes were few. Inside, the power seat that was standard in '94 was made an option; the options list also gained an electronic AM/FM stereo with CD player and premium sound. Seen here is the base convertible, which started at $20,795. *Bottom left and top, middle, and bottom right:* SVT issued a new race-ready Cobra R for 1995, this time with a 351 V-8 tuned for 300 street-legal horses. Only 250 were built, all white coupes with bulging fiberglass hoods and no weighty back seat or air conditioning. Sticker price was a hefty $35,499. *This page:* Famed automotive designer Larry Shinoda (who was responsible for the styling of the original 1969–70 Boss 302 Mustangs) developed the styling tweaks and special graphics for a limited number of aftermarket-modified "Shinoda Boss" Mustangs.

But the celebrating didn't end there. Again recalling Sixties doings, Ford got a special Cobra convertible named pace car for the '94 Indianapolis 500. Sure enough, Dearborn wasn't entirely conceding the power issue to GM, and by the end of the model year it had built 6009 new-design Cobras, 1000 of which were ragtops sold as replica Pace Cars.

Another SVT project, the '94 Cobra wore a unique front fascia, low-profile rear spoiler, 17-inch five-spoke chrome wheels with extra-wide Z-rated tires, discreet front-fender snake emblems, and a leather-lined interior with trendy white-face gauges. Underneath were bigger brakes with twin front calipers and standard antilock control, a GT suspension again made slightly softer for "controlled compliance" handling, and a 302-cid V-8 massaged for…240 horsepower. Motor-noters heaved more sighs. Even this new Cobra was still 35 horses shy of a standard V-8 Camaro/Firebird.

Car and Driver found the Cobra narrowed the performance gap with GM, but not much. Though its five-speed coupe clocked 0–60 in 5.9 seconds and the standing quarter in 14.7 at 96 mph, both times were a good half-second adrift of a Z28's. The Cobra "is undoubtedly the most muscular Mustang available," *C/D* concluded, "and at $21,240 for the coupe and $24,010 for the convertible, the most expensive. At those prices…we have a hard time imagining that a new breed of customers will be flocking into SVT showrooms [some 750 carefully selected Ford dealers]."

But if Mustang remained runner-up in a drag race, it still easily won the sales race. In fact, with model-year output of just over 137,000, the '94 Mustang came close to outselling Camaro and Firebird combined. Ford also built more ponycars for the calendar year: some 199,000 versus GM's 192,000. Only a bit less impressive, Mustang's showing marked a 16 percent gain on 1993, itself a good year despite the new GM competition.

Though little change was expected for '95, Ford expanded the herd at midseason with the GTS, essentially a GT coupe with base-model trimmings and a friendlier $16,910 price. The year also introduced a new limited-edition Cobra R coupe with a 351-cid V-8—Mustang's first since

Opposite page: Mustang power entered the modern era for 1996 with the adoption of Ford's overhead-cam 4.6-liter modular V-8s. GTs like this one ran a single-cam version with the same 215 hp as the last pushrod 302. Designed for future emissions standards, the new mill required extensive underhood changes to fit but was announced outside only by small front fender badges. That year's SVT Cobras switched to a twincam 4.6 whose 305 hp finally brought Mustang up to performance parity with larger-engine GM ponycars. This page: Mustang's segmented taillights changed from horizontal to vertical for '96, and the base V-6 got a five-hp boost to 150. The passive anti-theft system that debuted on the '96 GT and Cobra was made standard on 1997 base models like this convertible.

1973—borrowed from the hot-rod F-150 Lightning pickup. With 300 hp and 365 pound-feet, the new R looked a scorcher on paper, helped by a domed fiberglass hood and another stripped-out interior. But despite more power and less weight, it would only keep pace with an everyday Z28, C/D timing a so-so 5.4 seconds to 60 mph and a 14-second/99-mph quarter-mile. Perhaps it's just as well that only some 250 were built, again mainly for competition.

Mustang's headline news for 1996 was under the hood, which itself was changed. After 40 years of faithful service, the GT's pushrod V-8 was honorably retired in favor of Ford's "modular" 4.6-liter (281-cubic-inch) overhead-cam unit. The new iron-block, aluminum-head engine claimed no more power or torque, however, so performance remained on par with the '95 GT. But the 4.6 was smoother than the old "five-point-oh" and ran cleaner, too. It was also taller, prompting a bulged hoodline and structural changes in the engine bay. V-6 models got those too, plus five more horses

for 150 total. The only other visual distinctions were a mesh insert for the front air intake and—in a Sixties flashback—three-lens taillamps turned from horizontal to vertical.

SVT Cobras also went "mod" for '96, but they got a "premium" V-8 with aluminum block, forged crankshaft, specific *dual*-overhead-cam cylinder heads, and other upgrades. Horsepower checked in at 305, a solid 90 hp more than the sohc GT and 65 up on the '95 Cobra. Torque was 300 pound-feet, matching GM's hottest stock ponycars at last. Still, the twincam engine only leveled the playing field while changing the Cobra's character in a way some disliked. That's because it thrived on revs—"Anything under about 3500 rpm is bogging-down territory," said one tester—with relatively weak low-end torque that demanded liberal use of the mandatory five-speed gearbox. Still, a three-way *Car and Driver* showdown ranked the SVT ahead of a top-power Firebird Formula and just slightly behind a similarly optioned Camaro SS. The Cobra was "the best daily-driver muscle car,"

said the editors, "the one car we would most want to drive home at the end of a long day."

Despite the new engines, Mustang model-year production dropped a steep 27 percent for '96, skidding to 135,620. Cobras accounted for 10,006 of those units, the most SVT could turn out in a single year. The '97 lineup showed very few changes, but demand took another header, losing 20 percent year-on-year to close at 108,344, though Cobra volume stayed about the same.

Model-year '98 output jumped 62 percent to 175,522 units. Though that surely pleased Ford, the spurt was tough to figure, as changes were again modest. Engineers liberated another 10 horses from the GT V-8, bringing the total to 225. Performance was scarcely affected, but speed-seekers could now buy SVT-developed over-the-counter "off-highway" parts—including a supercharger kit.

In all, the 1994–98 SN95 must be judged a success, even though Mustang had long since become a niche product that couldn't hope to equal its enormous mid-Sixties popularity during an age in which trucks often outsold cars. But the Fox-4 pony was hardly ready for the glue factory—as we were about to see.

Opposite page, top and bottom left: Retuning took the 1998 Mustang GT's sohc V-8 to 225 hp, and all '98s got safer "depowered" airbags per federal decree. A rear deck spoiler was standard on both GT coupes and convertibles. *Top right:* SVT Cobras remained visually stealthy versus the more ubiquitous Mustang GTs, but got a new five-spoke alloy wheel for '98. *This page:* Ford's Windsor, Ontario, plant built the Cobra's twincam "mod" V-8, whose aluminum block was cast in Italy. The crankshaft was forged in Germany. At $30,200, the Cobra ragtop remained the priciest Mustang for '98. While slow sales had GM pondering the discontinuation of its Camaro and Firebird models, Mustang sales for 1998 were running 30 percent above '97 levels.

Ford's ageless ponycar was rejuvenated one more time for 1999 with "New Edge" styling, more power, and many key refinements. Though Dearborn soon ran into stormy weather, Mustang cantered into the new century with its fastest, most roadable models yet.

1999-2004: ON THE EDGE

Mustang marked its 35th birthday with an extensive 1999 makeover intended to keep the S95 design going a few more years. Described by *Road & Track* as "Ford's New Edge goes retro," the reskinned exterior sported crisp body lines, reshaped head- and taillamps, and a scalloped hood with nonfunctioning "sugar scoop." Simulated rear-fender air vents returned, front fenders gained nostalgic "pony tricolor" badges, and the grille's galloping horse was back in its traditional chrome "corral." But it wasn't all about visuals. Fully boxed chassis rails increased structural stiffness, and GT spring rates were recalibrated to improve handling.

More power was also on the agenda, and in useful doses. The 3.8-liter V-6 gained a sizable 40 horsepower to reach 190 total, thanks to a new intake manifold, freer-flowing cylinder heads, and low-friction pistons. It also added five pound-feet of torque, plus a vibration-damping "balance shaft." The 4.6-liter GT V-8 muscled-up by 35 hp to 260 via bigger valves,

higher-lift camshaft, freer-flow intake and exhaust, and other measures. A laudable new GT option was electronic traction control, which applied the rear brakes and/or reduced engine power to minimize wheelspin. It was a great supplement to the GT's standard antilock brakes (ABS, still optional for V-6s).

The rejuvenated '99s got a mostly thumbs-up reception. All models earned praise for melding a tighter driving feel and meatier steering with a more supple ride and less cabin noise. *R&T* pronounced the fortified V-6 "a respectable performer," while *Motor Trend* judged its manual GT coupe "as good or better than any stock Mustang we've ever tested...." The car dispatched 0–60 mph in 5.4 seconds, the quarter-mile in 14 at 100.2 mph.

Styling drew the most criticism. Design VP Jack Telnack had developed "New Edge" as both follow-on and antidote to his aerodynamic "jellybean" look that had been widely imitated and now seemed stale. But the

geometric lines fit uneasily on the SN95 bodies. *AutoWeek* likened the restyle as "akin to putting a baseball cap on a shoebox."

Buyers may have felt uneasy too, as model-year volume dropped by nearly a fourth from 1998 to 133,367 units. The "dot-bomb" debacle and other bad economic news didn't help, nor did higher prices: up $500 on V-6s, $900 on GTs, lifting the range to $16,500–$25,000.

An updated SVT Cobra coupe and convertible bowed a few months after mainstream models, with improvements all their own. New "tumble-port" cylinder heads and other tweaks lifted the twincam V-8 by 15 hp to 320 hp, the same as the top Chevrolet Camaro/Pontiac Firebird option. Traction control and ABS were standard here, joined by big new Brembo-brand disc brakes.

But the most talked about SVT feature was independent rear suspension. It consisted of high-rate coil springs, lower control arms, upper toe-control links, and a thicker antiroll bar. All mounted to a welded-up tubular subframe along with an aluminum-case differential and Cobra-

specific halfshafts. Cleverly, SVT engineered the entire setup for easy bolt-in on the assembly line.

Despite all this, the '99 Cobra was a puzzle. To be sure, the IRS erased 110 pounds of curb weight and 125 in unwanted unsprung weight, so the car was now more balanced and "pointable" than the live-axle GT. It was also less prone to bump-steer on softer springs that furnished a more compliant ride. But these benefits weren't usually manifest on the road and were hard to discern on the track. "Viewed in this way," said *Motor Trend*, "the SVT superpony seems hardly worth [its] extra $7000."

Testers also found the Cobra slower than 320 hp implied, and dynamometer tests revealed some 30 horses were indeed MIA. The explanation turned out to be a batch of defective intake runners and exhaust components from a Ford supplier. To its credit, SVT recalled all '99 Cobras on the ground for free repairs, but the effort took so much time that SVT had to skip the 2000 model. The team did, however, manage another Cobra R, this time with 385-hp *5.4-liter* V-8. It was the fastest

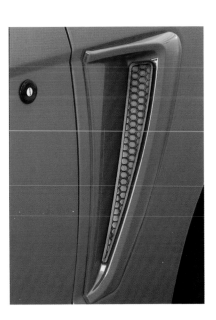

Opposite page, left: Mustang adopted Ford's "New Edge Design" theme for 1999, with fresh lower-body sheetmetal over the existing SN95/Fox-4 structure. Base coupes like this one started at $16,470; the $310 V-6 Sport Appearance Group added a rear spoiler, alloy wheels, and other sporty features. *Right:* Front fog lights and larger wheels mark this convertible as a GT. A V-6 coupe brings up the rear, but remained the top-selling model in the line. *This page:* Mustang's '99 restyle imparted a crisper, slightly huskier "retro" look, with new iterations of trademark elements like triple taillamps (top center), and simulated bodyside scoops (above right). A "corral" for the running-horse grille mascot returned (above center). Headlamps (top left) were reshaped. A new hood with nonfunctional scoop (above left) was standard for GTs, as were new-design alloy wheels (top right). All '99 Mustangs were considered 35th Anniversary editions, but special front-fender emblems were affixed only to base and GT models, not SVT Cobras.

factory Mustang yet, capable of 0–60 in under 5.0 seconds, a 13-second quarter-mile, and a stunning 1g of skidpad grip. The 2000 R was costly for a 'Stang at $54,995, but included a high-flying rear spoiler, deep front air dam, huge Brembo brakes, and genuine Recaro seats. Only 300 were built, all red coupes. They sold in a trice.

While the SVT episode played out, Ford happily observed Mustang's 35th birthday in April 1999, hosting huge gatherings at Charlotte Motor Speedway and in Southern California (as it had five years before). Ford also issued about 5000 GTs with a 35th Anniversary trim package marked by a raised scoop on a black-striped hood. At year's end, the U.S. Postal Service issued a stamp honoring Mustang as one of 15 American icons of the 1960s.

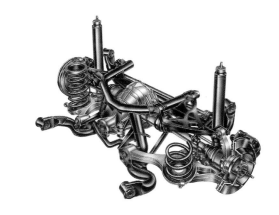

With the parties over, regular Mustangs saw predictably little change for 2000. Despite that and a worsening economy, sales turned up on a *calendar-year* basis, rising 4.1 percent to nearly 173,676.

The September 11 terrorist attacks temporarily depressed car sales across the board in 2001, so Mustang did well to record 169,198 calendar-year orders. Several encouraging developments helped. For starters, the Cobra returned with all 320 horses accounted for. *Car and Driver* put two on a dynamometer to be sure, then reeled off 0–60 mph in 4.8 seconds and a 13.5-second quarter-mile at 105 mph. Even better, *C/D* decided the

Cobra had "joined the ranks of competent sports coupes... Now you can point [it] exactly where you want and assume it will go there."

Only a bit less satisfying was the midyear "Bullitt" coupe, a specially equipped GT previewed by a year-2000 concept. It was the brainchild of J Mays, who'd come to Ford in late 1997 to succeed the retiring Jack Telnack as corporate design chief. Mays saw problems with the '99 styling and tried to "correct" them here, omitting the rear spoiler and adding a unique hood scoop, side scoops, rear-roof trim and rocker moldings, plus an aluminum fuel-filler flap. Inside were specific leather-covered seats, an

Opposite page: As expected, Mustang saw only minor alterations for 2000. V-6 convertibles started at $22,220, GT coupes at $22,440. *This page:* The street Cobra was sidelined for 2000 while SVT fixed an engine problem from '99. But in its place came a heroically winged new Cobra R. Packing a 385-hp 5.4 V-8, this purpose-built factory race car could do 0–60 in under 5 seconds, 13-second quarter-mile blasts, and a stunning 1.0g on the skidpad. A deep front airdam, Brembo brakes, deeply bolstered Recaro seats, and that high-flying rear wing were all standard. Just 300 were built, all red coupes.

This page: Mustang's star attraction for 2001 was the midyear GT-based Bullitt coupe, named for the classic 1968 movie starring Steve McQueen and a hot '68 fastback. Most of the 6500 built were finished in Highland Green just like the movie car, but black and True Blue were also available. Special features included aluminum interior accents, "retro" wheels, red brake calipers, and a muscled-up exhaust note. *Opposite page, left:* Here the 2001 Bullitt poses with an excellent replica of the original in front of the San Francisco sky-line. *Right:* Base models got standard 16-inch wheels instead of 15s, but Mustang was other-wise little changed for 2002.

aluminum shift knob and pedal trim, '60s-style gauge graphics, and chrome doorsill plates. The entire package paid homage to *Bullitt*, the 1968 cult film in which Steve McQueen raced a Mustang 390 fastback through the streets of San Francisco against bad guys in a Dodge Charger.

But the Bullitt was more than cosmetics. Upgrades began with the engine, which gained a larger throttle body, cast-aluminum intake manifold, smaller accessory-drive pulleys, and a freer-flow exhaust system. The result was 265 hp, only five more than stock GT, but with a slightly fatter torque curve and a noticeable difference in the engine's sound and feel. Ride height lowered by 3/4 inch combined with specific strut/shock units, antiroll bars, and what Ford called "frame rail connectors" to deliver the best ride and handling of any non-Cobra Mustang. Brawny 13-inch front brake rotors clamped by red-painted calipers gave first-rate stopping power.

The Bullitt cost $3500 more than a stock GT coupe yet was little faster. But it was fast to move out of showrooms, and dealers had no trouble

selling the planned 6500-unit one-year run at or above sticker price ($28,230). Most were painted Highland Green Metallic, like McQueen's movie car, though black and True Blue were available.

Motor Trend reported that the Bullitt was to be "the first in a series of short-term specials designed to bring extra excitement and collectibility into the current [line]." Excitement was surely needed for 2002. The Cobra was a no-show, and the only other news involved turning popular option groups into separate models with dull names: V-6 Standard, Deluxe, and Premium; GT Deluxe and Premium. Calendar-year sales duly dropped again, to 138,356, a worrisome 18.2-percent slide in a year when zero-percent financing had stoked the general market to red hot. The one consolation was GM's announcement that the Camaro/Firebird would be discontinued after '02

Mustang sales ticked up to 140,350 in calendar 2003, a happy happening for Ford Motor Company's centennial year. Two new sizzlers played a part. Arriving first, in spring '02, was an SVT Cobra packing a huge new supercharged wallop of 390 hp and 390 pound-feet. Accommodating the blower dictated numerous changes to the twincam V-8, including an iron block for durability under pressure, a water-to-air intercooler, new heads, and different pistons giving suitably lower compression (8.5:1). The only transmission was a Tremec six-speed manual, a legacy of the '00 Cobra R. The suspension was naturally retuned, and rolling stock was upgraded to inch-wider cast-alloy wheels with high-speed 275/40ZR rubber. Other modifications included a vented hood (to counter the blower's added heat), revised front fascia and rocker panels, an air diffuser beneath the back bumper, and a lower-profile spoiler. With all

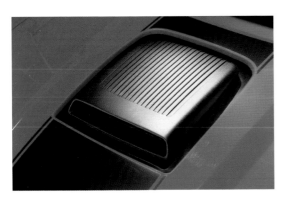

this, SVT's latest delivered near 2000 Cobra R thrust at a much friendlier price: $33,460 to start. The stats told the tale: 0–60 mph in 4.5–4.9 seconds, quarter-mile ETs around 13, 0.90g skidpad stick. Even so, *Road & Track* found the blower Cobra "refined enough for those who elevate performance and affordability…above ultimate sophistication."

Even more affordable was the Bullitt's 2003 follow-up: the first Mach 1 in 25 years. Another variation on the GT coupe, it carried an unblown Cobra V-8 tuned for 300 hp and topped by a functional "shaker" hood scoop straight from the Sixties. Pricing started at $28,705, a stout $3715 more than a GT Premium coupe, but the extra dough also bought a six-speed manual gearbox, slightly lowered suspension, Brembo brakes, unique exterior touches, and "comfort weave" leather upholstery. Reaction was fairly predictable. Despite a dated basic design, the revived Mach 1 was runner-up in a *Car and Driver* comparison with three high-tech import-brand sporty cars. Why? "Brute fun. Drop the hammer [and] 60 mph is yours in a

Opposite page: SVT went all out for 2003 by supercharging the Cobra's twincam V-8 to create one of the most potent street Mustangs yet. With 390 horses and 390 lb-ft of torque, both the coupe (below) and convertible (above) could run 0–60 in well under 5 seconds. Larger brakes and rolling stock helped control the formidable thrust. The shifter connected to a mandatory six-speed manual gearbox. A bulging twin-scoop hood was also new. The convertible shown here features the unique wheels and two-tone leather seats included with the $1495 Anniversary Package that Ford offered to commemorate 10 years of SVT performance. This page: An exclusive "Mystichrome" paint option was one of the few changes for the 2004 supercharged Cobras. It was a new high-tech finish that changed hue depending on ambient light and one's vantage point. The $3650 price included chrome alloy wheels, as shown here. The exotic paint made simple touch-ups a tricky, expensive process.

scalding 5.2 seconds...the fastest time in this test....Perhaps Henry Ford was wrong. History isn't bunk. It's a hoot."

History figured into three more blasts from Mustang's past for 2003. The GT-style V-6 appearance group was renamed Pony Package, recalling the popular 1965–66 option. Joining it later in the season was a $995 GT Centennial Package with two-tone leather interior, mandatory black paint, and special badging. A similar ensemble made up a $1495 Cobra 10th Anniversary group for the SVT.

Still, the trusty old steed was obviously marking time, and everyone knew a frisky new filly was on the way. Ford heralded the next Mustang in January 2003 by unveiling a pair of "modern retro" concepts—an eye-grabbing convertible and fastback coupe, at the Los Angeles and Detroit Auto Shows.

The SN95 thus made one last run for 2004. Pundits didn't expect much change—and didn't get it. Still, the Mach 1 added 10 horses and V-6 models

three, and the Cobra offered striking "Mystichrome" paint—a high-tech finish that changed color with ambient light and/or the viewer's vantage point—as an exclusive $3650 option.

But wasn't 2004 Mustang's 40th birthday? Yes, Ford said, despite its longtime inconsistency on whether the first one was a "1964½" or an early '65. No matter. This observance involved an option group for Premium models that combined the Interior Upgrade Package with unique wheels and special trim while deleting the stock rear spoiler. All very low-key for such a milestone event, but announced in time for another: On November 20, 2003, a 40th Anniversary ragtop came off the Dearborn line as Ford Motor Company's 300-millionth vehicle.

It was a fitting tribute to Mustang in general and the successful SN95 design in particular. But now Ford was finally ready with another new ponycar—only this one really *would* be new.

Opposite page and this page, above: Mustang marked its 40th birthday with a modest $895 Anniversary Package for base and GT premium models. Though 2004 would be the last gasp for Mustang's long serving Fox platform, the trusty steed made one final historic splash when a 2004 GT convertible rolled out of the Dearborn assembly plant on November 20, 2003, as the 300-millionth Ford Motor Company vehicle. Chairman and CEO William C. Ford Jr. came by to help celebrate the milestone. *Right:* Premiere Mustang tuner Roush Performance cooked up its own Fox-Mustang send-off with a limited run of 40 high-performance 440A Mustangs. The name decodes like this: 400 hp, 40th production year, anniversary edition.

Mustang was reborn for 2005 with an all-new "heritage" design that rekindled the warmest feelings about a 40-year love affair. Inside and out, the '05's masterful styling drew more from classic Sixties Mustangs than ever before but retained a modern, cutting-edge feel.

2005-2009: RETRO REVIVAL

The faithful SN95 might have been replaced for 2001 or '02, but steady Mustang sales again prompted Ford to take its time with a ponycar redesign. The time was well spent. Developed as project S197, the truly new 2005 was everything Mustang lovers had hoped for—and more.

Styling, finalized under design manager Larry Erickson and design VP J Mays, was a "retro" tribute to classic Mustangs, yet thoroughly modern and distinctive in its own right. Tellingly, there were no intramural design contests for S197, and the only consumer clinics were held at Mustang club events. "We did one [styling prototype]," Mays told Consumer Guide®. "We knew what we wanted."

Engineers, led by Hau Thai-Tang, ended up developing an essentially new unibody architecture for S197, the first specific to Mustang. One reason was a change in production venue from the old Rouge plant to AutoAlliance, the joint-venture Mazda-Ford facility in nearby Flat Rock,

Michigan. The move was supposedly made for the sake of improving quality and to align build costs more closely with sales. A solid rear axle continued, mainly because Mustangers said they preferred it over an independent suspension.

The '05 arrived sharing some 35 percent of its components with other Dearborn products, but it wasn't obvious. The most extensive use of computer-aided design in Ford history also saved money while allowing closer coordination among development-team members. Engineers spent over a year fine-tuning some 6000 variables in road-tests from Arizona to Sweden, plus a nonstop 24-hour grind at Ohio's Nelson Ledges racetrack.

The new-millennium Mustang launched in late 2004 with four fastback coupes: V-6 Base and V-8 GT in Deluxe and Premium versions. Lower-priced Base Standards joined in for 2006. Base models exchanged the old pushrod 3.8 V-6 for Ford's familiar 4.0-liter overhead-cam unit, tuned for

210 horsepower and 240 pound-feet of torque. The single-cam 4.6-liter "mod" V-8 continued for GTs, but acquired new heads with three valves per cylinder, variable cam timing, and a computer-controlled variable-intake system that promoted more efficient combustion. These and other measures added 40 hp for a total of 300, not impressive for the day but a new high for a mainstream Mustang. Torque also improved, swelling 13 pound-feet to 320. Both engines gained electronic "drive-by-wire" throttle control as a means of reducing emissions and fuel consumption. A revised five-speed manual gearbox was standard with both mills, but the optional automatic was now a five-speed too.

To the engineers' credit, S197 ended up larger but little heavier than SN95, coupes scaling 3300–3500 pounds. Wheelbase stretched nearly six inches, to 107.1, which not only enhanced appearance but made for more-even front/rear weight distribution (53/47 percent) and thus better handling (abetted by wider tracks). Overall, S197 stood 4.4 inches longer than SN95 (at 187.6), 1.4 inches taller (54.5), and 0.8 inch wider (73.9). Most interior dimensions expanded as a result, but this was still a two-adults-plus-two-kids car.

Though decidedly quaint for a 21st-century car, the solid rear axle was well controlled via twin lower trailing links, a single upper link, and a lateral Panhard rod. Coil springs continued at both ends, as did standard antiroll bars. Struts reprised at the front, but were now located by L-shaped lower arms, while springs remounted from the arms to the struts gave a more precise feel to the power rack-and-pinion steering. All models came with four-wheel disc brakes. ABS with traction control remained standard for GTs, available for V-6s. Serving "passive safety" were newly optional front side airbags providing head/torso protection.

Convertibles joined the new coupe herd in spring 2005 with the same trims and standard equipment. The tightest, most solid-feeling ragtop Mustangs ever, they boasted a fully lined power fabric roof with compact "Z-fold" mechanism. Convertibles got slightly softer suspension tuning in the interest of ride comfort, yet handled nearly as well as coupes, with

Opposite page: Under heritage-conscious design chief J Mays, Mustang's design direction shifted to a modern reworking of vintage forms. This full-size clay from early 1999 was a two-sided model. Its left half showed an evolution of the 1999–2004 car. The shape and dimensions of its right side would be honed over the next few years into the 2005 Mustang. *This page, top left and right:* Mustang's new platform would bear the S197 code, and designers used its dimensions to underpin this full-size clay from September 1999. The study had many features that survived in some form to the production car. These included a bodyside "scoop," pronounced wheel arches, and grille-mounted fog lights. Triple-element taillamps and a big decklid badge would also endure the design gauntlet. But this proposal also held some dead ends, such as the rear side windows and marker lights integrated with the headlamps. *Above:* The S197's side-window shape paid allegiance to that of the '67–'68 fastback, as this '67 GT makes clear.

Opposite page: With the development of the 2005 Mustang well along in secret, two 2003 concept cars provided a hint of what was coming. Built on the chassis of the Lincoln LS and Thunderbird, the concept coupe and convertible fueled speculation that this so-called DEW98 platform would also underpin the new Mustang. Created by Ford's California design specialty shop, the show cars were actually customized versions of the virtually completed S197 body. *This page:* Camouflaged development "mules" were subjected to cold-weather work in Sweden, 24-hour endurance runs on racetracks, and countless trials at Ford's proving grounds.

crisp turn-in, modest cornering lean, and poised, predictable moves.

Although the 2005 Mustang looked a surefire hit, even Ford was surprised when calendar-year sales jumped 24 percent from '04 to 173,273 units—and were mostly won without profit-draining incentives. Indeed some early buyers willingly paid well over sticker. Not that pricing was an issue for most people. As ever, Mustang offered terrific bang for the buck. The V-6 coupe started under $19,000, the GT coupe at around $25,000. Equivalent ragtops ran some $4800 more.

Inevitably, a few things were sacrificed for affordability. Most every road-tester cited cut-rate interior materials, and the "new" V-6 was actually a very old design with nowhere near the refinement of most rival engines. There was also carping about ergonomic details, steering both too light and too quick for best control—and the usual rear-axle hop under full power, though it was less irksome than before.

But no car is perfect, and the new Mustang's virtues made it easy to forgive its vices. *Car and Driver* lauded a V-6 coupe for doing a brisk 6.9 seconds 0–60 mph—with *automatic*. The magazine later chose a GT coupe over Pontiac's reborn GTO, even though the Ford trailed in 0–60 (at 5.1 seconds) and in the quarter-mile (13.8 at 103 mph). "[T]he Mustang wins because...it makes the most of what it has, doesn't suffer for what it doesn't have, charges you less than you'd expect, and beckons [you to] take it home."

Sales rose to 178,632 for calendar 2006 despite predictably few product changes. GTs added extra-cost 18-inch wheels, and an optional Pony Package returned for Premium-grade V-6s, bundling ABS and traction control with GT visuals.

Mustang was not a factor in a new financial crisis that had come to a head at Ford Motor Company, which was now fighting to survive after years of losing market share and tons of money. This partly reflected the ill-advised new-century expansionism of president Jac Nasser, who took Ford into costly sideline ventures and overpaid to acquire four prestigious European automakers. Greatly alarmed, chairman William C. Ford Jr., old

Henry's great-grandson, took over as president, but soon realized the need for a more-dynamic day-to-day leader. After much deliberation, the young scion hired veteran Boeing executive Alan Mulally in late 2005. Besides moving to dispose of Nasser's acquisitions, Mulally stunned the industry by mortgaging most company assets—even the Blue Oval logo—for $23.6 billion to keep the doors open and fund a recovery plan based on fresh products and a vastly streamlined business model. Though a huge gamble in 2006, Mulally's boldness paid off when the economy tanked in 2008, triggering America's worst recession since the 1930s and forcing Chrysler and General Motors to seek government loans under bankruptcy. Avoiding the taint of "bailout" only accelerated Ford's recovery, and by 2010 the company had turned the corner, posting a $6.56 billion profit, the highest in 11 years.

Mulally was just taking charge when Ford's Special Vehicle Team

Opposite page: The 2005 Mustang hit showrooms in late 2004. Overall, the new model was 4.4 inches longer than the '04, on a wheelbase stretched by 5.8 inches. Rear quarter windows evoked bygone styling while giving light to the rear seat and aiding driver vision. A chrome Mustang galloped on every grille, but only the V-6 model showed the emblem on the combination trunk lock/badge. *This page:* Grille-mounted foglamps, a rear spoiler, dual exhaust tips, and 17-inch wheels were GT-exclusive features.

released a potent new S197-based Cobra for 2007. The name, however, was Shelby GT 500, as Carroll Shelby himself assisted with development, having recently renewed ties with Dearborn as an advisor on the mid-engine Ford GT supercar. This new project was spearheaded by none other than Hau Thai-Tang, who'd been promoted to director of Advanced Product Creation and head of SVT.

Save a tasteful lack of phony air scoops, the new GT 500 channeled the macho looks of the 1967–'68 originals with a specific "powerdome" hood and aggressive face, a rear spoiler, rocker-panel stripes, unique interior trim, chrome cobra logos in the usual places and, as an option, dorsal "LeMans" striping. Lurking within was a supercharged 5.4-liter twincam V-8, basically the 550-hp Ford GT unit with a less-expensive Roots-type blower and "milder" tuning that nevertheless yielded a thumping 500 hp and 480 pound-feet. This muscle was too much for any automatic on Ford's shelf, so the only transmission was a heavy-duty six-speed manual, familiar from recent Cobras and the winning FR Mustangs developed by the Ford

Opposite page, top: Convertibles joined their coupe kin in spring 2005. GT ragtops started at a $30,745 in top-line Premium trim. *Bottom:* Aftermarket manufacturers had a field day with the new Mustang, offering a smorgasbord of body kits, wheels, and other customizing goodies. *This page, left and bottom left:* The racing-inspired Mustang GT-R concept's front fascia hinted at the styling of the forthcoming Shelby GT 500. *Bottom right:* Racers wasted no time putting the 2005 Mustang into service. Pictured here is a lineup of Grand Am Cup competitors at Virginia International Raceway.

This page, top left: "Legend Lime" was an especially striking color in the factory Mustang palette. *Top right:* Shades of '66: Hertz again offered a specially trimmed Shelby for rental in the 2006 GT-H. *Left:* A new-for-2006 Pony Package outfitted V-6 Mustangs with special trim that included a nostalgic grille bar. *Opposite page:* Though it was a bit too avant-garde for mainstream American tastes, the Italian-designed Giugiaro Concept was evidence of Mustang's international appeal.

Racing division. Thrust control also dictated a beefed-up suspension, big Brembo disc brakes with 14-inch four-caliper rotors up front, and sticky high-performance tires sized at 255/45ZR18 fore, 285/40ZR18 aft.

Performance was predictably impressive. *Car and Driver* reported the best published stats: 4.5 seconds 0–60, 12.9 for the quarter-mile. *Automobile* accurately portrayed the new GT 500 by saying it "goes fast, stops well, corners hard enough to scare dates, and should be comfortable to live with on a daily basis." Pricing was also fairly comfortable: $45,755 for the ragtop and $40,930 for the coupe, the latter undercutting Chevrolet's new Corvette Z06 coupe by a whopping $28K. Trouble was, the 'Vette was noticeably quicker and more dynamically composed, though Ford was already working to even those scores.

The main news among regular 2007 Mustangs was availability of heated front seats and, for GT Premiums, a nostalgic California Special (C/S) Package with bodyside scoops and other unique trim, plus 235/50ZR18 tires on polished alloy wheels. Ominously, Ford's well-publicized troubles

and a deteriorating national economy began wreaking havoc on car sales. Mustang didn't escape, falling 25 percent for calendar '07 to 134,626. That total includes GT 500s, which were built at AutoAlliance. The model was planned for a three-year run (2007–09) of 10,000 units, but actual production was probably far less.

Mustang sales plunged 32 percent in 2008, to 91,251, despite the addition of two more models. One was a new Bullitt, actually a package option for the GT Premium coupe that was trimmed and equipped much like the '02 original. Major attractions involved a cold-air induction system that lifted the 4.6 V-8 from 300 hp to 315, plus a different, great-sounding exhaust system. Also included were a mandatory manual gearbox, tighter final-drive ratio, uprated suspension and brakes, "mag-style" wheels, and unique trim inside and out.

The other '08 addition was Ford's riposte to the Corvette Z06: the GT

This page, top: Yet another resurrection of a name from Mustang's past, the 2007 GT California Special Package cost $1895 and included hood and bodyside scoops, stripes, and 18-inch wheels. *Left:* The 2007 Shelby GT Mustang packed 325 hp and was available only in Performance White or Black. *Opposite page:* A truly muscular revival of the classic Shelby GT 500 was unleashed as a 2007 model. A supercharged 5.4-liter V-8 with a hair-raising 500 hp ensured that the new model would handily outperform the original. The GT 500's classy, leather-lined cabin was also the luxury king among factory-built Mustangs.

This page: Mustang went Hollywood again in 2008 with a reprise of the Bullitt Mustang (top left) and a starring role as "KITT" (top right) in the short-lived revival of the *Knight Rider* TV series on NBC. The TV KITT car was a tricked-out Shelby GT 500KR; civilian KRs (left) boasted 540 hp, unique suspension, and a carbon-fiber hood with scoops patterned after the original 1968 GT 500KR. *Opposite page, left:* The 2008–'09 "Warriors in Pink" trim package served as a fund-raiser for breast cancer awareness and research. *Right:* A novel panoramic glass roof was a new option for 2009.

500KR. Yup, a new "King of the Road," but coupe only this time. SVT pulled out all stops, starting with a special cold-air intake system and recalibrated engine electronics that boosted the "blown" 5.4 V-8 to 540 hp and 510 pound-feet. To handle the added power, all chassis components were retuned and a front strut-tower brace installed (shades of the classic Boss 429). SVT also applied functional brake-cooling ducts, and Goodyear contributed specific-compound Eagle F1 Supercar tires. Exotic lightweight carbon-fiber was used for a hood with working scoops and vents, as well as for a unique aerodynamic front splitter and even door-mirror housings.

For all that, the KR only narrowed the performance gap with the Z06, and Chevy had upped the ante for both acceleration and handling with its 638-hp Corvette ZR1 (new for '09). But if still not truly sports-car nimble, the fortified Shelby was hardly slow. One magazine reported 0–60 in 4.4 seconds and a quarter-mile of 12.6 at 119 mph. It was hardly cheap, either, at $120,000 to start, the costliest production Mustang ever. But none of this mattered much, because the KR was planned as a very-limited edition and only 1712 would be built. Of these, 1571 were sold in the U.S., including

1000 specially trimmed 40th Anniversary '08s. The remainder went to Canada and various export markets. These, too, were built at Flat Rock alongside regular GT 500s, which continued.

Meanwhile, the nation's economy continued going from bad to worse. So did Mustang sales, calendar-2009 volume slumping another 27 percent to 66,623 units. The lineup was virtually unchanged, but that was less a factor in the dismal sales result than high unemployment, a public mood both angry and pessimistic, and particularly the widespread lack of ready consumer credit brought on by The Great Recession.

But a few faint signs of recovery were starting to appear, and the S197 Mustang was about to get a major two-step freshening as if to hasten the return of happier days. It was pure coincidence, of course, but a welcome development all the same.

The 2005 Mustang's boffo sales sent General Motors and Chrysler scurrying to revive their own dormant ponycar nameplates. With the re-introduction of the Dodge Challenger and Chevrolet Camaro, Mustang finally had direct competition again. Ford responded with a raft of styling, engineering, and quality improvements that made for some of the best Mustangs ever.

2010-2012: RIVALRIES RENEWED

Suddenly, it was 1970. Or so it seemed in 2009, as Mustang faced its first direct competition in seven years.

The instant-hit S197 undoubtedly encouraged Chrysler and General Motors to proceed with planned revivals of the Dodge Challenger and Chevrolet Camaro, respectively. Both new ponycars were previewed as concept cars in 2006, but were slow to reach customers, the Challenger rolling out for 2008-09, the Camaro appearing in early '09 with 2010-model coupes. The delays partly reflected the fact that Chrysler and GM were drowning in debt, due to the same long-standing problems that forced Ford to seek financial lifelines in 2006 (see Chapter 11). This partly explains why Mustang's reborn rivals were essentially cut-down two-door versions of weighty midsize sedans; neither automaker could afford all-new designs that would likely generate only modest sales. (Chrysler and GM were in such dire straits that they surrendered to bankruptcy in

mid-2009, accepting government-brokered reorganization in exchange for desperately needed taxpayer bailout funds.)

With that, the rejoined ponycar battle pitted two Clydesdales against a quarter-horse, a disparity noted in most all media reports. But it's telling that the smaller, lighter Mustang won many comparison tests simply by being judged the most fun to drive. Though it wasn't tops in every performance stat, the S197 endeared itself to journalists—and many enthusiasts—for remaining truest to the mid-1960s ponycar idea. "Perhaps it's because the Mustang stayed in production while the others took long sabbaticals," ventured *Car and Driver* in July 2009. "Ford used the intervening years well. This [2010] Mustang is the most beguiling yet."

Ford, of course, had learned of its competitors' plans well in advance and had prepared to defend Mustang's turf. Accordingly, the 2010 models received significant styling changes and much-improved interiors for a

sales launch in spring 2009—just in time for Mustang's 45th birthday. (No commemorative specials, though.) The 2011s bowed the following spring with new engines as the main event. Buyers responded to this rejuvenating, and calendar-year sales turned up in 2010, rising nearly 11 percent, to 73,716. The 2011 story was still unfolding as this book was being prepared.

Besides a "faster-looking" pony emblem, the 2010 restyle changed all lower-body sheetmetal to impart a leaner, more muscular look. Some saw echoes of 1970 in the base and GT models' newly rounded nose, slimmer grille, pulled-back headlamp clusters with inboard turn signals, and Shelby-like domed hood. The tail, too, was slightly tapered in overhead view, and a newly canted back panel cradled larger taillamps with sequential turn signals a la late-1960s Thunderbirds and early Mercury Cougars. Exterior dimensions were virtually unchanged, but the reskin trimmed air drag by 4 percent on V-6 models and by 7 percent on V-8 GTs. The Shelby GT500 combined most of these changes with a revised scoops-and-vents hood and a slightly meaner rendition of its aggressive face.

Opposite page: Mustang got a substantial revamp for 2010 that included restyled bodywork and a much-upgraded interior. Highlights of the new body design included a fresh grille emblem and a convex rear fascia. Reshaped taillights had sequential turn signals similar to 1960s Thunderbirds and Mercury Cougars. *This page:* Shades of 1970! Eye-grabbing Grabber Blue rejoined the Mustang color palette for 2010, and could be spiced up even more with optional rocker-panel stripes. The base Mustang's 210-hp 4.0 V-6 was carried over from 2009.

Interior changes were arguably more dramatic, and certainly welcome. Though the basic cabin design was much as before, acres of hard, shiny plastic and faux-metal trim gave way to soft-touch, low-gloss surfaces and genuine aluminum accents for a far classier look and feel. In addition, the dashboard was reworked to accommodate a navigation system with an 8-inch central touch-screen that also controlled some audio and climate functions and displayed images from an available rearview camera that activated on shifting into Reverse. Related to this was another first-time Mustang option, Ford's new Sync system. Developed with Microsoft, Sync provided voice-control for most "infotainment" features, plus wireless connectivity for cell phones and digital media players. Like comparable systems at other automakers, it enhanced driving safety by minimizing the need for manual adjustments of the new electronic toys.

All 2010s received a number of technical updates. Electric-motor steering assist replaced the traditional belt-drive hydraulic pump, chassis

components were recalibrated, and standard wheel diameters grew an inch (to 17s for V-6 models, 18s for GTs, 19s for Shelby coupes). Mustang's 4.0-liter V-6 was basically untouched, as were the five-speed manual and automatic transmissions. GTs, however, graduated to the 315-horsepower 4.6 V-8 of the 2009 Bullitt with the same cold-air induction system. The GT500KR was no more, but "regular" Shelbys inherited its 540-hp 5.4-liter supercharged engine.

Ford's Advance Trac stability system with traction control was now standard across the board. Drifting fans applauded its full-off mode, as well as normal and intermediate "track" settings. Manual-shift GTs offered a new "Track" package with less-intrusive stability intervention, plus stiffer springs, thicker antiroll bars, premium 255/40ZR19 Pirelli PZero "summer" tires, twin-piston front brakes, and a 3.73:1 limited-slip rear axle to replace the stock 3.31 or available 3.55 open diff. Last but not least, all 2010s were quieter inside, thanks to tighter build tolerances and extra

sound insulation. Ford playfully took advantage of this to give GT models an "induction sound tube" that ran from the intake plenum to the cabin so occupants could better appreciate the V-8's joyful noises.

The 2010 Mustangs earned critical plaudits for their fresh styling, greater refinement, and more-upscale interiors, plus suspension tweaks that made handling a touch more buttoned-down. In these respects, the five-year-old S197 was on par with the brand-new Camaro and Challenger. The carryover powertrains seemed a disadvantage on paper, with less V-6 and V-8 horsepower and a manual gearbox with only five speeds instead of six. Yet real-world performance was surprisingly close, thanks largely to Mustang's considerable weight advantage: a sizable 300 pounds lighter in manual V-8 coupe form than the 6.2-liter Camaro SS, and a whopping 560 pounds trimmer than the 5.7 Hemi Challenger R/T. Test results said it all. *Car and Driver*, for example, timed 0–60 at 4.8 seconds for the Chevrolet, 4.9 for the Ford, and 5.1 for the Dodge. Respective quarter-mile results were 13.0 seconds at 111 mph, 13.6 at 105, and 13.6 at 106. Despite this, Mustang returned the best observed fuel economy with 17 mpg versus

This page, top left and right, and left: The Shelby GT500 was beefed up for 2010 with a supercharged 540-hp 5.4 V-8. Even the shift knob had racing stripes. *Bottom:* Mustangs were quite popular in Grand-Am road racing. Here, the #11 car of David Empringham, Scott Maxwell, Tom Nastasi, and David Russell takes a practice lap for the 2010 Rolex 24 at Daytona. *Opposite page:* Roush Performance added a host of performance and appearance upgrades to the stock Mustang GT to create the menacing 435-hp 427R.

This page: Mustangs were little changed on the surface for 2011, but both base and GT models got fantastic new engines. Despite their retro styling touches, Mustang interiors were as high-tech as any competitor's; upscale available features such as a navigation system with real-time traffic updates, Ford's Sync voice-command, and a rearview camera provided state-of-the-art functionality and convenience. *Opposite page:* Mustang's new V-6 was a healthy 3.7 that boasted an impressive 305 hp while achieving a 30-mpg EPA rating on the highway; it easily outclassed the previous V-6's 210 hp and 24 mpg highway rating.

14–15 for its rivals. If Ford's pony was still this competitive with old engines, what could it do with new ones?

As noted, the 2011s duly answered that question with two fully modern powerplants, plus new Ford-built six-speed transmissions to go with them. The replacement V-6 was the 3.7-liter (227-cubic-inch) unit familiar from recent Dearborn products like the Lincoln MKS premium-large sedan. Reengineered for the rear-drive Mustang, it arrived with 305 hp and 280 pound-feet of torque, nearly as muscular as the previous GT V-8 and up 95 hp and 40 pound-feet from the ousted 4.0.

But it was the new V-8 that had everybody talking. Developed under the code name Coyote, it restored the hallowed "5.0" badge to Mustang front fenders with a 4951cc displacement—a new 302. Against the final 4.6, horsepower shot up by nearly 100 to 412, torque by 65 pound-feet to 390. That was on premium fuel; using regular dropped the numbers to 402 and 377, still pretty good. The Coyote and the 3.7 V-6 engines both featured weight-saving all-aluminum construction, port fuel injection, and twin

This page: With V-6 Mustangs getting such a substantial power upgrade for 2011, V-8 Mustangs couldn't stand pat—and they most certainly did not. Their all-new 5.0 liter V-8 made 412 hp, yet was EPA-rated at 26 mpg on the highway. Mustang enthusiasts rejoiced at the return of the celebrated 5.0 badge, as well as the neck-snapping performance and spine-tingling exhaust note of the new motor. *Opposite page:* GT Premium ragtop models topped the non-Shelby Mustang lineup with a starting price of $38,695. A "401A Rapid Spec Premier Trim and Color Accent Package" added cool pony badges on the door panels and "racing stripe" seats for a reasonable $395.

overhead camshafts operating four valves per cylinder via Ti-VCT, Ford's new Twin Independent-Variable Cam Timing system, effective on both intake and exhaust sides.

Ford said the Coyote shared nothing with the old "mod" V-8 except a few bolts and cylinder bore-center spacing. The latter allowed using the same basic manufacturing setup, thus saving money, and also helped chop a full 12 months from the development schedule. *Car and Driver* noted specific output of 83 hp per liter versus 64 for the Camaro's pushrod 6.2 and 70 for the Challenger's pushrod 5.7 Hemi. Even so, this V-8 seemed destined for even more power and a long, distinguished career. As *C/D* also observed, "Should the need for more power arise, Ford has future-proofed the Coyote engine for applications such as supercharging and direct [fuel] injection."

The Ti-VCT powerplants restored Mustang's performance parity with Camaro (the heavyweight Challenger wasn't really in the hunt). Comparing manual-shift V-6 coupes, *C/D* clocked 0–60s and quarter-miles of 5.4

seconds and 14 at 104 mph for Mustang and 5.9 and 14.5 at 99 mph for Camaro. Manual V-8 versions tied on 0–60 at 4.6 seconds. Mustang trailed slightly in the quarter-mile, but was discernibly quicker in the telling 30–50 and 50–70 sprints. When it was all over, Mustang won the dual duels by fairly healthy point spreads. The editors termed the 2011 V-6 "a mostly brilliant product [that] can satisfy just about anyone" and the Coyote-powered GT "an almost unmitigated delight." Other showdown tests reached similar verdicts.

The Shelby GT500 wasn't overlooked for 2011, gaining a new aluminum-block 5.4 supercharged V-8 that took a critical 100-plus pounds off the front end. Torque was unchanged at 510 pound-feet, and horsepower only inched up to 550, but the updated engine returned better EPA fuel economy, allowing this Shelby to escape the government's gas-guzzler tax for the first time. It also made performance even more ferocious. *C/D*'s manual coupe clocked 0–60 in 4.1 seconds (versus 4.5 for a 2010), 0–100 in 9.1 (9.6), and a 12.4-second quarter-mile (12.7). No less important, stops were

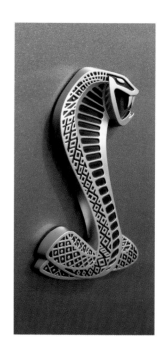

This page: The 2011 Shelby GT500 got an aluminum engine block in place of an iron block, a 10-horsepower boost (from 540 to 550), and other minor updates. This example is equipped with the $3495 SVT Performance Package. *Opposite page, top:* Professional drifting driver Vaughn Gittin Jr. teamed up with Ford Racing Performance Parts and aftermarket manufacturer Classic Design Concepts to create the Mustang RTR. The $7895 package delivered a variety of performance and appearance upgrades inspired by Gittin's own Formula Drift Mustang race car. *Bottom:* Hip-hop star Nelly poses in front of the one-off 5.0 coupe customized for him by *DUB Magazine*. Ford dealers also offered a 2011 DUB Edition V-6 Mustang with special trim, 20-inch wheels, and a blacked-out look similar to Nelly's own ride.

shorter, skidpad grip was higher at 1g (previously 0.91), and understeer was greatly reduced. Aiding the cause on C/D's tester was a newly optional SVT Performance Package with higher-rate springs and shocks, slightly lower ride height, and wider, stickier Goodyear Eagle F1 Supercar "G:2" tires on inch-larger alloy wheels (19s fore, 20s aft). Despite its racy moves, the SVT-equipped Shelby was a perfectly civilized daily-driver, as Consumer Guide®'s editors learned first-hand. Two final changes involved standard high-intensity headlamps and, for the coupe, an available glass roof panel, a regular-Mustang option since 2009.

If not exactly cheap at $49,495 to start, the 2011 GT500 wasn't overpriced, considering it matched or beat the performance stats of costlier cars like the Corvette Grand Sport and BMW's vaunted M3. Other models also maintained Mustang's high-value tradition, laudable given the many worthwhile 2011 improvements and inevitable price creep. Stickers

Both pages: Ford revived the hallowed Boss 302 monicker for 2012 on a Mustang that was truly worthy of the name. Development testing for this track-ready Mustang occurred at California's storied Laguna Seca road course. The Boss 302 V-8 was a seriously modified, high-revving 5.0 that redlined at more than 7000 rpm and delivered 444 hp. Exclusive Boss 302 ten-spoke wheels recalled the look of the classic Minilite racing wheels on the original Boss 302 Trans-Am cars. Mustang chief engineer Dave Pericak (pictured opposite) and the rest of the Mustang team went to great lengths to make sure that the new Boss lived up to the legacy of the 1969–'70 originals…and bested the lap time of the $58,000 BMW M3 coupe around the Laguna Seca track. They succeeded at both goals.

(including destination) ranged from $22,995 for the base-trim V-6 coupe to $32,845 for the Premium GT version. Convertibles ran $5000 more model for model. Even so, and despite lacking ragtops, Camaro outsold Mustang in 2010 by some 7600 units (at 81,299).

But Ford was already plotting to put Mustang back in front of the sales race. Indeed, spring 2011 ushered in two limited-edition showroom lures as early-2012 models: a reborn Boss 302 and the Boss 302 Laguna Seca. Each was essentially a track-focused but street-legal version of the stock six-speed-manual GT coupe and developed with assistance from none other than Parnelli Jones, who, with George Follmer, drove original Boss 302s to win the 1970 Trans Am team championship.

Upgrades for the 21st-century descendant began with the new Coyote V-8, which received special intake runners, reprofiled camshafts, more-aggressive engine electronics, and a freer-flow exhaust system—a slick "quad pipe" setup with twin four-inch outlets at the rear and sneaky side outlets that exited in front of the rear wheels. The result was 444 hp and peak torque of 380 pound-feet. A separate "TracKey" ignition

key activated completely different PCM (powertrain control module) software to optimize throttle response, cam timing, fuel delivery, throttle-off deceleration, and other parameters for weekend competition sorties. Chassis changes were equally extensive: high-rate springs, five-way-adjustable front shocks, reduced ride height, larger rear anti-roll bar, specific 19-inch wheels with Pirelli PZero treads, and a heavy-duty version of the stock GT's available Brembo-brand brake package. The electric steering, ABS, and stability control were all reprogrammed to suit, and a short-throw shifter was installed. Outside, the "base" Boss 302 was decked out with nostalgic bodyside C-stripes, a deeper front spoiler, and an add-on rear spoiler. The cabin sported the expected special trim—and 11 fewer pounds of sound insulation. The only extra was a package combining genuine Recaro front seats with a Torsen limited-slip differential.

That option was standard for the Boss 302 Laguna Seca, which boasted a more-aggressive aero body kit lifted virtually intact from the $79,000 Boss 302R turnkey racer (announced in late 2009 for a planned 2010 run of just 50 units). The "super Boss" also featured specific wheels, tires, and

chassis calibrations, plus a rigidity-enhancing cross-brace instead of a rear seat and a contrast-color band around the grille.

The "base" Boss 302 was priced at $40,145; choosing the Laguna Seca edition tacked on another $6995. Both were planned as limited-production models with a total run of 4000, 750 of which would be the "race car with a license plate" Laguna Seca version. If history repeats itself, we wouldn't be surprised to see a slightly updated Boss 302 appear for 2013.

It's not hard to imagine that Ford will spring more happy surprises before it sends the S197 into honorable retirement and brings forth a brand-new ponycar that will surely be timed for Mustang's milestone 50th birthday in 2014 or '15. Though the next-generation design remains a mystery at the moment, recent history suggests it will be every inch a Mustang, with all that implies, yet fresh and exciting in its own right.

Meantime, here's a toast to the one and only Original Ponycar and to Ford Motor Company for sticking with it through good times and bad. It's been a great ride, filled with wonderful memories. But the future beckons, and we can't wait to see what's next.

Opposite page: For hardcore racing enthusiasts, Ford offered the Boss 302 Laguna Seca Edition, which came standard with Recaro seats, a dashtop gauge pod, and a chassis-stiffening X-brace instead of a rear seat. Other serious hardware included front disc-brake cooling ducts and a not-quite-street-legal front air splitter that was sure to scrape on any speed bump or steep driveway. *This page:* Shelby American, Inc., continued to produce a range of specially modified Mustangs for 2012. Pictured clockwise from top left are the 800-hp (!) GT500 Super Snake, the GT350 convertible, and the GT350 coupe hustling through a turn aside its legendary ancestor, the 1965 Shelby GT350.

INDEX